TOP SECRET

TOP SECRET

THE DICTIONARY OF ESPIONAGE AND INTELLIGENCE

Bob Burton

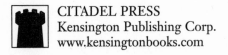

CITADEL PRESS
Kensington Publishing Corp.
www.kensingtonbooks.com

CITADEL PRESS BOOKS are published by

Kensington Publishing Corp.
850 Third Avenue
New York, NY 10022

An earlier version was first published in a hardcover edition by Paladin Press, Boulder, Colorado.

All Kensington titles, imprints, and distributed lines are available at special quantity discounts for bulk purchases for sales promotions, premiums, fund-raising, educational, or institutional use. Special book excerpts or customized printings can also be created to fit specific needs. For details, write or phone the office of the Kensington special sales manager: Kensington Publishing Corp., 850 Third Avenue, New York, NY 10022, attn: Special Sales Department; phone 1-800-221-2647.

CITADEL PRESS and the Citadel logo are Reg. U.S. Pat. & TM Off.

First printing (updated edition): February 2005

10 9 8 7 6 5 4 3 2 1

Printed in the United States of America

Library of Congress Control Number: 2004113763

ISBN 0-8065-2650-5

Dedicated to Lesley Koelsch of Santa Barbara, California

Lesley's dedication to the pursuit of arcane terminology and insider slang of one of the more "close held" professions in the world's history made all this possible.

Lesley now rests in peace . . . an eternal peace, yet she will be long remembered by her friends and love.

God bless you, Lesley.

CONTENTS

FOREWORD

The elite professions of our society—law and medicine are the second and third worst offenders—have since the beginning developed their own vocabularies, called *cants*, so that ordinary people can't understand what they're talking about.

The worst offender in this area is what is euphemistically known as the "intelligence community." My dictionary defines "community" as "sharing, participation and fellowship."[1] The one thing intelligence people do not do is share, and frankly, they're not big on participation and fellowship, either.

If your life depends on as few people as possible knowing what you are doing, you have a tendency to keep your mouth shut. And when you're talking to people you're working with, to use a cant that no one else understands.

The result of this is that when many—perhaps most—writers write about what I consider the most elite profession of them all, intelligence, they have no idea of the cant.

To solve this social problem, Bob Burton has compiled this tome.

Who is Burton to do this?

Every once in a great while, Hollywood actually makes a film about the world few people know or talk about that doesn't cause intelligence people to snicker all the way through it. One such film was *Proof of Life* starring Russell Crowe. By the time Crowe, playing the role of an ex-SAS officer trying to get back an American kidnapped by Latin American guerrillas, was ready to go after the bad guys, I was on the edge of my seat.

When Crowe rappelled down from a chopper into the jungle, I said aloud, "Go get 'em, Burton."

From his days as a member of the Marine Corps' Force Recon to his status now as one of the World's Better Bounty Hunters and Hostage Rescuer emeritus, and without question the most respected man in counterespionage, Bob Burton has been there, done that, and has the T-shirt.

And going against what I said before about fellowship, Bob Burton has made friends—and kept them—with the heavy hitters in just about every intelligence agency in the world, from our CIA and FBI to Mossad and MI6 . . . and a host of others.

I was talking one time to a Medal of Honor winner at a Special Operations Association reunion in Las Vegas when Bob walked in with G. Gordon Liddy.

"My God," the Medal of Honor recipient said, in awe, stopping in midsentence. "Isn't that Bob Burton?"

And these people contributed to this book, explaining in detail what certain terminology meant, and where it came from, about subjects they wouldn't talk about to anyone else.

I'm now writing a novel about intelligence. An early version of *Top Secret* is five inches from my keyboard, and will be there until I finish.

Thank you, Bob Burton.

—W.E.B. Griffin
Life Member, Special Operations Association
Honorary Life Member, Special Forces Association

ACKNOWLEDGMENTS

Any book of this nature depends upon the goodwill of many people in sensitive positions. Often, security precautions will create an overly security-conscious mentality, guarding even the jargon and terminology of the trade.

In accumulating these entries I had to earn and communicate goodwill to the various security officers, active and retired, that I dealt with.

Special thanks must go to Mr. Jack Mathews, a former senior official with the CIA. Mr. Mathews was instrumental from the beginning of this book to the final pages in assisting me with some of the almost unverifiable words that I ran across. Thanks are also due to Mr. Richard Gookin, associate chief of protocol with the US Department of State for assistance on the expulsion procedure of a captured foreign espionage agent.

Special thanks must also go to the many active duty officers of the various intelligence agencies alluded to in this book. Their wish to remain nameless will be honored but they shall not go thankless.

A mystery was cleared up for me by Mr. Donald Stigers, chief, Security Branch, Office of Intelligence Support, Department of State, regarding the Bureau of Intelligence and Research. Many thanks to Mr. Stigers. The security officers at several foreign embassies proved helpful with words belonging to their own services and clarification of in-house slang. They wish to remain nameless and will be so honored. Ultimate responsibility, however, remains on my shoulders for any and all errors.

Introduction

Few professional groups have developed their own language as eclectically as has the intelligence-gathering community—the spies, spooks and espionage agents. The intelligence community has borrowed terms from the computer industry, the space program and the legal, medical and scientific professions, and has given them new meaning. Such words and phrases as *compromise, crypto, HUMINT, ELINT, source, sourced, TOP SECRET, COSMIC TOP SECRET* and *topographic crest* are all used in daily conversation by the men and women that make up the agencies and military organizations charged with the tasks of learning our enemies' secrets and preventing hostile forces from learning ours. These terms come from the military-spy-science connection of the Office of Strategic Services, the Special Operations Executive and other intelligence and paramilitary operations of World War II.

Conversely, much of the intelligence trade's semantics has entered the civilian community. *Cover* and *cover story* are now suspected by most parents when their child arrives late for dinner with a plausible excuse for his tardiness. And, of course, the child feels *burnt* by the parents.

The language of the analyst may differ from that of the field officer, the "spy," only in that each would have his own terminology within the structure of the intelligence agency. In management, the career officer, desk and control will each have some terminology of his own. And let us not overlook the *singleton*, the agent who works alone.

While each facet of the intelligence agency must be aware of the others' linguistic nuances in order to communicate, the Directorate of Science and Technology will have some words that won't readily be recognized by the other CIA directorates or operations.

This, however, is not exclusively a book of CIA jargon. The special disciplines of codes and ciphers, special operations, and high-risk security have been incorporated throughout the pages.

Special operations, a very *special* kind of warfare, will be having more and more of its lexicon on the front page of America's newspapers in the coming years, with the new emphasis on American unconventional warfare (UW). I have tapped as many UW terminology sources as possible.

I have made no attempt to attach each word to a particular discipline, for the words are readily interusable. Neither have I made any pretence at offering this book as the final word on these entries. I have found that approaching three intelligence officers on certain esoteric words produces three different definitions. Unlike the code and cipher groupings and the military's special operations terms, many of the "spy" jargon entries have never before been put on paper. When I found a "spy" jargon word from a 1940 spy book, I checked with current contacts within the intelligence community to see if it was still being used. Those that confirmed its use were at a loss to come up with a book definition, yet knew vaguely how it was used. A word such as *buck slip* would fit the description.

Many words that I could not verify or corroborate were left out. Dated terminology from World War II was not included, but words still in usage from World War II can be found here.

I tried to find those words that enjoy contemporary use and were from the areas I tried to touch upon: espionage and the intelligence community in general; security; special operations or unconventional warfare; and codes and ciphers. Within this framework are a vast number of words constantly changing in meaning. Those words represented here are of a "now" nature except where noted.

Beyond the terminology of the trade, I have included several appendices which offer a bit more insight into the intelligence community. I hope these will whet the appetite of the reader for further study of that misty defense that we call the intelligence community.

And if no other purpose is served, I hope this book gives a "personality" to those dedicated individuals who are constantly on guard protecting this nation's security.

TOP SECRET

Abdul Negative or pejorative expression for a Muslim or Arabic enemy. Variation of Abdul Majeed, one who serves a glorious man. Negative usage: "Get a load of those Abduls . . ." Modestly traced to Russian usage during early Afghanistan war of 1980s.

abort Mission failure, usually for reasons other than enemy action. The mechanical snafus of the Iran raid of April 1980 are a good example. In intelligence circles, to abort is to cease all activity in the early stages of establishing an intelligence operation or network. An operation is usually aborted because of a security flap.

Abwehr The German intelligence service during World War II; highly efficient. Toward the end of the war, Hitler purged its staff and leading factions, including Admiral Canaris, the chief, for pro-Allied feelings.

access The ability or opportunity to obtain classified information. There are various levels of authorized access; someone with a SECRET clearance, for example, will not have access to TOP SECRET information. Access is sometimes unauthorized: Someone may have access to a document because of a security failure.

access, classified document Confirmation of the prior clearance of an individual to documents of a certain level.

access document An authorization granting access to an individual for certain classified or protected documents, matter or devices. Sometimes the document must be signed by the grantee, and a secrecy oath might be required to obtain this authorization.

accountable cryptomaterial Cryptomaterial which, for reasons of control or security, requires periodic accounting to the office of record and issue from the time of receipt until the time of disposition.

accountable document control system A system of formal records and receipts used to control the following types of material: TOP SECRET; SECRET; restricted data; NATO, SEATO, and CENTO classified material; classified proposal information; cryptographic information (regardless of classification); classified foreign documents; and material marked *special access required*. Other material, such as an item marked *proprietary* by private industry, may be receipt controlled.

acepromazine An animal tranquilizer used covertly on humans via a knife, syringe, etc.

active measures Soviet term for covert action, disinformation and other active forms of propaganda.

active opposition The counterintelligence service of the target country. In Teheran, for instance, the active opposition would be Iranian counterintelligence. Throughout the world the Soviet KGB would formerly have been the active opposition, especially in the more underdeveloped Third World countries.

additive A number or series of numbers or letters added to code, cipher or plain text to encipher it. The additive is often referred to as *the key*.

administrative cryptoaccount An account established for holders of cryptodocuments that will be used for reference purposes only and is not operational in nature.

administratively confidential A term used in the White House and in various administrative departments for a sensitive matter that might cause embarrassment if leaked or compromised. It is not a security classification.

ADP system security Includes all computer hardware/software functions, characteristics and features: operation procedures, accountability procedures and access controls at the central computer facility; remote computer and terminal facilities; and the management constraints, physical structures and devices. The term also refers to personnel and communications controls needed to provide an acceptable level of protection for classified information to be contained in an automatic data-processing system.

ADSO Dated CIA term for *assistant director for special operations*, used before the creation, in 1948, of the CIA Office of Policy Coordination. Both terms refer to the chief in charge of clandestine operations.

Aeroflot A Soviet national airline, often a front for KGB and GRU activity. KGB officers can be found on the staff of most Aeroflot in-tourist offices.

Agency, the Well-used expression for the CIA. "He worked for the agency." Sometimes emphasis is placed on *the*.

agent An individual, usually a foreign national, who acts under the direction of an intelligence agency or security service to obtain, or assist in obtaining, information for intelligence or counterintelligence purposes and/or to perform other intelligence functions. An employee of the CIA is always referred to as an officer. A CIA officer supervising agents would be a case officer; the agent is the *local* assisting the CIA officer. An FBI employee is also called an agent.

agent assessment Reports sent to Langley, Va. (the current CIA headquarters), on the "back channel" on a timely basis assessing an agent's performance in order to continue to justify his pay to headquarters. *See* back channels.

agent development Development of a social or professional relationship with an individual with demonstrated access to a target in order to determine if he could be induced to engage in an operational relationship to provide classified information on a continuing basis. The case officer may assign the task of agent development to a PA or agent. *See* agents, CIA, principal agent.

agent of a foreign power   A circa World War I term, still in use. *See* persons of interest.

agent recruitment   The pitch made to an individual who, after development by a PA or agent, is considered ready to undertake a clandestine relationship for the purpose of providing intelligence on the target to whom he has access.

agent termination/disposal   This evil-sounding term simply refers to the firing of an agent. The severance fee is determined by how much he knows and how much trouble he can cause if he talks. The agent's relationship with his case officer and his hopes for future employment will also determine his demands at the time of firing.

agents, CIA

action agent   An agent usually hired by a PA or case officer for a one-time operation typically involving violence, explosives or some other kind of action.

agent   A spy that works directly under the PA and engages in intelligence collection or covert action operations. In the interests of security, he is separated from other agents under the control of the PA.

agent-Bolvan   Slang from Moscow Center, loosely interpreted as *dummy agent*. Essentially the same as a notional agent in purpose, an agent-Bolvan is used to divert a hostile intelligence service from a sensitive operation.

agent in place   Often used to describe a defector believed by the United States to be more valuable in-place, at the post or position from which he wants to defect. The goal here is continued access to and conveyance of sensitive information. With luck the defector is allowed to defect before the opposition's counterintelligence realizes it has a mole, or penetration.

agent of influence   This person may or may not be on the payroll of the CIA. Generally he is an anticommunist official of a country in which the Agency is interested. He may be a local businessman, or even a journalist. All agents of influence have access to influential officials and media leaders.

agent provocateur   An old spy term for an agent or officer who, as a plant, is ordered to associate himself with a certain target group or suspected person with whom he must pretend to sympathize. The goal is the inciting of the suspect or target group into some action that will bring about apprehension or punishment.

career agent   Someone who is paid to collect and deliver sought-after information. This arrangement could last over many years, during which time the career agent's case officer may change.

contract agent   Sometimes called a *one-time agent*, the contract agent may be hired several times over a period of several years for various projects, such as muscle, intrigue and organization.

notional agent   A nonexistent agent used as a ploy or fiction by an intelligence organization in a deception operation. The notional agent ploy may be used in a false or dummy message to pull the opposition off the tail of a real agent or officer.

principal agent (PA)   An agent recruited and trained by a CIA case officer in all aspects of clandestine operations and communications. The PA is expected to spot, recruit and train other agents, which he then directs against specific intelligence targets selected by his case officer.

secondary or subagent   An agent who serves under the PA.

secret agent   A person acting clandestinely as a spy.

support agent   An agent recruited by the PA or agent to rent safe houses, cars, post office boxes and so on, and to undertake other tasks as required in support of a specific intelligence operation.

AGILE project   A special project run by Advanced Research Projects Agency in Vietnam to develop anti-guerrilla equipment. This equipment included radios, shoes, weapons, clothing and load-bearing gear (knapsacks, rucksacks). Hence AGILE: Anti-Guerrilla Insurgency Light Equipment.

Agitatsiya   Office of Agitation and Propaganda. Old Soviet directorate for political and procommunist propaganda, especially in literature, drama, music and art.

agitprop   Agitation and propaganda, especially in the cause of communism. This term was first used in the early 1930s by *Newsweek* magazine.

Air America   The airline used by the CIA to support its paramilitary operations in Southeast Asia, specifically in Laos, Cambodia, Vietnam and Thailand.

air intelligence   Formerly air combat intelligence. This term applies more to naval intelligence air operations than to US Air Force.

alert memorandum, alert memo   A document circulated among analysts, technical services people or operatives, alerting them to the possibility of information or intelligence, opposition, events or defectors; or a memo sometimes attached to reports or briefings alerting the reader to certain points. Often used to put the Agency on record as having first raised the alarm of an impending crisis, the alert memo puts top administration on notice for emergency action.

American Black Chamber   A top-notch group of cryptologists put together by Herbert Yardley in the 1920s. The Black Chamber, America's first serious attempt at code breaking and enciphering, was broken up by Secretary of State Stimson who believed, naively, that "Gentlemen do not read other gentlemen's mail."

anagram   Transposition of the letters of a word or sentence to form a new word or sentence.

analysis   *See* Appendix 3: The Intelligence Cycle.

apparat   Soviet word. The entire agent network deployed against a specific intelligence target.

area assessment   In unconventional warfare, the collection of specific information prescribed by the commander to commence immediately after infiltration. A continuous operation, area assessment confirms, corrects, refutes, or adds to intelligence acquired prior to infiltration from area studies and other sources.

area command   In unconventional warfare, the organizational structure established within a UW operational area to command and control resistance forces. Usually, it will integrate the Special Forces operational detachment and the resistance forces.

area divisions   Geographical divisions delineated by CIA for control of operations. *FE/Plans* stands for Far East (Division) Plans; *WH/Ops* Western Hemisphere Operations; and *FE-3* refers to a specific branch within the division: here, branch 3 of the Far East Division.

area study   In UW, the prescribed collection of specific information pertaining to a given area, developed from sources available prior to entering the area.

Artamonov, Nikolai   Russian defector who came over in 1959 and eventually worked for the Defense Intelligence Agency (DIA). His cover name was Nicholas Shadrin.

Originally questioned as to his bona fides, he was eventually allowed access to secret work. In 1966 the KGB approached him in Washington, possibly not knowing he was a defector in the first place. The FBI then turned him into a double agent by letting the KGB think he was willing to work for them. He disappeared in Vienna in December 1975. Was he originally a defector, or a plant by the KGB? His wife thinks he was killed by the KGB after they got him to Vienna. Some intelligence officials believe, however, that he was a mole all along, and that he had never really left the KGB.

assets   A term generally used to describe the friendly contacts in a given area who are willing to assist the United States. In general, any asset to an operation, usually a human information source.

atropine   Organic poison of the Belladonna family, tasteless, it attacks the central nervous system in five to eight minutes.

authentication   A security system or measure designed for communication systems to prevent fraudulent transmissions.

authentication equipment   Equipment designed to provide security against fraudulent transmissions and imitative communications deceptions or to establish the authenticity of a transmission, message, station, originator or telecommunications system.

authentication system   A cryptosystem or a cryptographic process used for authentication. A series of codes or ciphers that only the authorized would be familiar with.

authority to classify   That authority given to determine the value of documents and matter incidental to the national defense, and to place classifications on such data. TOP SECRET authority rests with less than seventy people in the United States, SECRET encompasses perhaps several thousand, and CONFIDENTIAL even more. Authority of classification is spelled out in an executive order that most presidents issue within a month or two of taking office.

authorized persons   Those persons who have been cleared for the receipt of classified information. Responsibility for determining whether a person's duties require that he possess or have access to any classified information, and whether he is authorized to receive it, rests upon the individual who has possession, knowledge or control of the information involved, and not upon the prospective recipient.

B

back channels   The secret and secure communications network maintained by the CIA at all embassies. Designed to circumvent normally used State Department frequencies, it is used when the cable traffic is clandestine and must be secured. Getting something done on the back channels refers to bypassing the routine procedures and going directly to the target or object.

backstopping   The process of creating a solid background for an officer working with a cover. In the past it was not unusual to use a legitimate, ongoing business as the cover. The officer would be carried on its payroll, and only the principal or owner of the business would know his new book salesman in East Europe was a CIA operations officer. If questioned, the firm would backstop, or back up, any inquiries.

backstopping, cover Reference backup for the undercover officer. Even when he is applying for something as mundane as credit, the cover staff at his "business number" will verify all that the officer put on the credit application. Usual covers are state, agriculture and economic departments, but civilian businesses are also used. *See* central cover division.

backstopping, flash Identification good only for the most cursory examinations—a driver's license for instance—flash backstopping is used on occasions when just "flashing" an I.D. is enough. Such an occasion could be getting a motel room in a phony name or opening a bank account. Flash backstopping will not stand up to deep investigation by the opposition.

Beardless Barbara Nickname of a New Jersey woman by the name of Barbara Ines Collins who broadcast English-language propaganda for Fidel Castro starting in May 1961.

Berlin Tunnel A major intelligence undertaking by the CIA in the mid-1950s. The Berlin Tunnel ran under the border between the Soviet and American zones in Berlin. At the Soviet, or East Berlin, end of the tunnel was a major junction of telephone and communications cables. These were tapped by the Agency. This tap was finally "discovered" by the Soviets in April 1956. Apparently, the Soviets knew of the tunnel from its planning stages via the plant, or defector in place, British officer George Blake. The Soviets allowed the operation to continue in order to protect Blake and keep his real allegiance secret until he finally "came over."

bigot list A very closely held list of cleared personnel that have access to a roster of foreign nationals (agents) under contract to the Agency.

bioaparat Russia's center for bioweapons research and manufacture.

Bi-Weekly Propaganda Guidance A booklet issued by CIA divisions to the CIA stations to update them on important events throughout the world from a CIA viewpoint. The CIA thought its stations should be aware of the CIA stand so that CIA-generated media propaganda would appear to reflect independent world opinion.

BKA-Bundess Kriminalamte The Federal Criminal Investigation Office. German equivalent of Britain's Scotland Yard or the United States' FBI.

black-bag work Originally, the movement of unvouchered funds, transported by diplomatic pouch or "black bag," to support agent operations; more recently, breaking and entering, although a professional does more entering than breaking. Black-bag work generally entails the planting of bugs or surveillance devices. Most agencies forbid it without a court order, despite its value.

black box Any inanimate or technical spying device, such as an electronic recording mechanism or a recording device on a commercial US aircraft.

black designation A designation applied to all wirelines, components, equipment and systems that handle only encrypted or classified signals; and to areas in which no unencrypted, classified signals occur.

black list A compilation of any kind of sensitive and compromising information or intelligence, especially a list of hostile agents in a given target area.

black mind One who is capable of seeing beyond the obvious or even the not-so-obvious. This is definitely a compliment when used in reference to a clandestine or covert action officer.

black operations Operations untraceable to the sponsor agency; any operation or project that is untraceable due to misrepresentation or disguise so that the originating party remains unknown. The Guatemalan coup of 1954 is a classic example of black work. Of course, by definition most black operations are outside the realm of discussion.

blind zone In the world of electronic countermeasures, an area where echoes cannot be received.

blow back Negative publicity or repercussions from an operation. This can be from either a successful or failing operation; usually the results are unanticipated or the reaction is stronger than previously thought possible.

blown Exposed; as in "the operation (project, cover) was blown by the Soviets (or the US media)." From common street usage. *See also* dirty, dirtied.

blue books Slang for the National Intelligence Estimates.

Board of National Estimates A division of the CIA that produced general estimates of world events that filled a need in the entire intelligence community.

Boehme equipment   A device automated for ongoing sending and receiving of code.

bona fides   Background verification, as in "Did you check the new defector's bona fides?" It is tedious work, sometimes taking years, to prevent a mole from penetrating an intelligence organization. Background verification would apply when the defector went to work for the country of refuge intelligence service.

book message   Policy changes relating to intelligence or covert-action operations that are electronically sent to field installations, stations and other scenes of ongoing operations.

bound documents   Books or pamphlets the pages of which cannot be removed without mutilation or damage. The binding must be that generally used by the book-binding profession, that is, either sewn or glued. Bound documents do not include those bound only with staples, brads, wire or other easily available commercial fastenings.

brainwashing   A system of psychologically "cleansing" the mind in order to purge an adversary of "unclean thoughts." Credited to the Chinese Communists after they seized control of China, brainwashing was used to change enemies of the regime into allies. The Chinese method is less brutal than that of the KGB; however, despite the academic cuteness of the name, brainwashing is fraught with terror. The goal is to break the subject's spirit by means of physical deprivation, and then to coerce him into adopting a communist viewpoint by rewarding his cooperation with such benefits as food and better conditions. Usually the effects are transitory for those who manage to escape a communist environment.

branch   A subunit or division within the CIA, usually smaller than a division and specifically zeroed in on a special section of a given area.

branch lines   A British term for contacts developed in the course of investigation or operations. Someone or something noted but not yet exploited.

breaktime   The time it takes to break down the resistance level of a subject in an interrogation of a brutal nature—usually five to seven hours.

Brigade 2056   Famous unit composed of Cuban exiles that landed on the shore of the Bay of Pigs in 1961. The brigade was trained by the CIA and paramilitary professionals and named after soldier number 56, who died in training. The designation *2056* was made to confound any opposition as to the actual number of brigades.

brush pass   A clandestine meeting in a public place for the purpose of secretly delivering information. What would appear to an untrained observer to be the accidental collision of two pedestrians on a crowded street or in a bar is really two agents, or officer and agent, passing valuable information. Usually, no words are spoken, although sometimes in a life-threatening situation, one may warn the other despite rules to the contrary.

buck slip   A note used to send documents from one CIA office to another.

bugging   Clandestine surveillance of a target; specifically, the use of electronic devices to eavesdrop in order to covertly monitor a conversation.

Bureau of Intelligence and Research   The State Department's primary liaison with other members of the intelligence community. Known by the initials *INR*, it is an effective intelligence-gathering member of the intelligence community.

burn, to be burned   To expose an opposition intelligence officer. A CIA officer may burn a KGB officer or, worse, the reverse may occur. Many times, when the opposition is too active, too aggressive, or has breached some unwritten treaty, an effort will be made by the CIA to cause embarrassment or expose the target KGB officer in a way that will cause his ejection from the host country. Normally, the KGB and CIA had a pretty good idea who the opposition officers were. In order to avoid the wholesale ejection of each side's officers by the host country, some limits of behavior are observed. The same is true with killing, assassinations and officer terminations. It would be a very expensive proposition if KGB and CIA officers killed each other, and so a necessary truce was adhered to here as well.

burn bag or burn basket   Depository for classified matter and documents that are to be destroyed by shredding or burning.

burst transmission An entire message is sent in a few seconds, often denying access to the message by those trying to intercept.

bury To conceal or hide certain words, phrases or messages in the text of a transmitted communication.

C

cables Those messages (telegrams) sent to CIA headquarters by the hundreds on a daily basis from CIA station chiefs.

cadre A UW, guerrilla warfare and paramilitary term denoting a nucleus of trained personnel capable of assuming command/control and training others.

cake or death An unspoken but soon realized ultimatum that a prisoner of spook war soon understands as his personal fate. Cooperate or die, which is presented in a subtle manner by the interrogator. Also slang within the intel communities for lessor confrontations as well.

CampX A Canadian location for Brit, US and Canadian operatives used during World War II and the Cold War.

candidate material   Material referred to collectively as *special nuclear materials* and *nuclear weapons*.

caption code   In cryptography, a code in which the phrases are listed under separate headings based upon the principal word or idea in the entire phrase.

case officer   A title for an intelligence officer engaged in the conduct of intelligence, counterintelligence and covert action operations in a foreign country. A case officer is also called a "control officer" or "agent handler."

case-study methodology   The generally accepted method used by intel agencies to train future spies. This method is specifically designed to revisit hundreds of cases to study the failures and successes in a case-by-case scenario.

Catherwood Foundation   A CIA cover foundation for funding operations that ran until the late 1960s. Ostensibly located in Bryn Mawr, Pennsylvania, the Catherwood Foundation was used to assist pro-American candidates wherever free elections were held, especially in the Far East. Effective in the Philippines, it was also used in Malaysia, Indonesia and Hong Kong, as well as other parts of the world.

cell   One of the lowest and most expendable of all espionage units.

Center, the (Moscow Center)   Moscow headquarters of the Soviet espionage establishment. It was composed of two sections: the KGB, responsible for all but military intelligence (but not prohibited from collecting it); and the GRU, the military intelligence directorate of the general staff of the Red Army. The KGB was the more powerful of the two entities, as its superiors ran the country.

central cover division   That unit of the CIA (and other agencies) that provides cover backstopping in the event someone tries to verify the credentials offered by an intelligence officer. A fictional business will be acknowledged on the phone, and the officer's employment at "Acme Painting" will be verified. Many phones will be within reach for the cover officer, and by reference to the central registry he will know which officer is being checked by the phone number.

central office of record   The Department of Defense or other user agency that requires accounting, receipts or reports for registerable COMSEC (communications security) material on a particular contract or project.

certificate of destruction   A certificate given to the person or office that brings classified matter to the officer in charge of destruction of classified material by shredding or burning. It is the user's receipt that the material has been destroyed as ordered. The certificate safeguards the superiors who ordered the destruction. The intermediary will surrender the certificate of destruction and will be given a receipt for it.

chad type   A special code tape for teletype operations, usually a five-unit code perforated for quick and easy separation.

chain of custody An administrative method of tracing the course that a classified document requiring signature security takes; used as a safeguard against compromise or carelessness.

CHEKA Russian acronym for *Extraordinary Commission for Combating Counterrevolution and Sabotage*, the first name given to what was known as the KGB.

ChiCom Early term for Chinese Communist. It is still used, but dated.

chief of station The officer in charge of a CIA station. Generally referred to as *the COS*. Immediate superior is the ambassador. Often, however, the ambassador will abrogate all interest or control over the station's affairs. Many ambassadors, in fact, have an "I don't care what you do, just don't tell me" attitude.

CI Group Formed by President Truman on 22 January 1946 and controlled by the National Intelligence Authority (NIA) founded at the same time, the Central Intelligence Group was seen as a grudging admission by Truman that an entity was needed to regulate and collect intelligence. Rear Admiral Sidney Souers was the first director, followed by Lieutenant General Hoyt Vandenberg in June 1946. On 26 July 1946 the National Security Act was passed and the CIG became an independent department called the Central Intelligence Agency.

CI nicks An old term for Central Intelligence nicks. *Nick* is slang for detective or investigator, fallout from the old book, magazine and radio series *Nick Harding, Counterspy*.

CIA's Secret War Military operations funded and organized in Laos in late 1958 through 1962. Operation White Star involved several hundred US Army Special Forces personnel under command of the late Colonel "Bull" Simons. White Star's objective was to thwart communist efforts to take Laos. L'Armee Clandestine recruited Meo and other Laotian mountain tribespeople, who rallied around their military leader, General Vang Pao. *See* White Star.

cifax The cryptography of facsimile signals or enciphered facsimile signals.

cipher A system of assumedly random and arbitrary symbols representing units or groupings of letters of the alphabet. *See* code.

cipher alphabet A list of equivalent letters used to transform plaintext to cipher or secret communications form. For example:

Plaintext:	A	B	C	D	E	F	G	H	I	J	K
Cipher Text:	R	B	K	P	E	T	D	P	W	O	A

cipher device Usually a hand-operated implement for enciphering or deciphering messages, for example, a hand-operated code wheel.

cipher machine Any machine or mechanical implement used for encoding or enciphering.

ciphony The cryptography of telephonic communications; enciphered speech signals. Ciphony involves the scrambling of voice communications by altering the current carrying the voice.

circuit discipline Proper use, transmission, monitoring, remedial actions, etc., of equipment communications, etc. Awareness of what is being said over what.

Civil-Military Advisory Commission (CMAC) A group composed of local citizens with military and police representation that participates in the internal defense and development (counterinsurgency) planning activity of the area coordinating center. This is a current phrase of special operations counterinsurgency.

Civilian Irregular Defense Group (CIDG) Known throughout Vietnam by its initials, CIDG (pronounced Sid Gees), this mercenary force was composed of ethnic Lao, Chinese and mountain tribesmen and Vietnamese employed by the CIA and Special Forces against the Viet Cong (VC) and North Vietnamese Army (NVA). Led mostly by US Army Special Forces, it was a very effective weapon against the enemy as well as a counterinsurgency unit.

civision The cryptograph of television signals or enciphered television signals. Reception is possible only with a descrambler.

clandestine mentality That much sought-after mind capable of planning and conducting clandestine operations.

clandestine operations Activities for the purpose of intelligence and counterintelligence sponsored or conducted by governmental departments or agencies in such a way as to ensure secrecy or concealment.

clandestine services A general reference to the "secret intelligence services" that would include, but not be limited to, the CIA, National Security Agency and Defense Intelligence Agency.

classification The privacy rating that all official information requires in the interests of national defense. The classification of a piece of information offers a specific degree of protection against unauthorized, or even inadvertent, disclosure.

classification authority The authority vested in an official of a user agency to make an initial determination that particular information requires protection against unauthorized disclosure in the interests of national security.

classification categories Unclassified, CONFIDENTIAL, SECRET and TOP SECRET.

classification guide A document issued by an authorized initial classifier to prescribe the level of classification and appropriate declassification procedures for specified information that is to be classified on a derivative basis. Guides are provided to contractors via DD form 254 and are titled "DoD Contract Security Classification Specifications."

classified Any documents, matter or material that has received a certain level of protection by being classified as to its sensitivity as defined in an executive order.

classified contract   Any contract that requires or will require access to classified information by the contractor or his employees in the performance of the contract. A contract may therefore be classified even though the contract document itself is not classified. A classified contract is used in private industry and is generally a result of a purchase order by the US government.

classified information   Any official information, including foreign information, that requires protection in the interests of national defense and that has been so designated by those with authority to classify.

classified matter   Any information, material or thing that has to be safeguarded in the manner and to the extent required by its importance, such indications being: CONFIDENTIAL, SECRET and TOP SECRET.

classifier   Similar to above "classification authority"; one who makes a classification determination and applies a security classification to information or material. A classifier may be a classification authority or may derivatively assign a security classification based on a properly classified source or according to a classification guide.

clearance   An official determination of eligibility for access to classified material, information or documents. Clearance will be rated CONFIDENTIAL, SECRET AND TOP SECRET. Specific classifications apply to each level of a user's access and are in relation to his duty.

cleared insider   Someone with clearance and a need to know.

close held Describes a project whose nature allows only "management" handling with little data going "downstairs."

closed areas Controlled areas created to safeguard classified material, which because of its size (e.g., a jet fighter) or nature cannot be protected by other means.

CNWDI When you see these letters, watch out! They designate TOP SECRET RESTRICTED DATA that might reveal the theory of operation or design of the components of a thermonuclear or implosion fission bomb, warhead, demolition munition or test device. Specifically excluded is information concerning arming, fusing and firing systems; limited life components; and total contained quantities of fissionable and high-explosive materials by type. Among the excluded items are the components that Department of Defense personnel, including contractor personnel, set, maintain, operate, test or replace.

code According to David Kahn, author of *The Code Breakers*: "There is no sharp theoretical line between codes and ciphers; [yet, a] useful distinction is that code operates on linguistic entities, dividing its raw material into meaningful elements and cipher does not."

code book A book or other document containing plaintext and code counterparts systematically arranged.

code group A group of letters, numbers or both assigned in a code system to represent a plaintext message.

code name An alias used by a spy for security reasons. Agents hired by case officers have code names to protect them, and code names are usually used on communications for security. Projects and operations are also given code names, usually in all caps, such as Project CAMELOT. *See* cover name.

code word A word that expresses a certain prearranged meaning beyond its face value.

coding delay The interval of time between transmission of the loran master (the transmitting machine at the cipher station) and the slave stations (the receiving stations).

coding room, code room The room or building, compartment or facility where coding and ciphering are done.

CODRESS Any transmission or message with the address buried in the encrypted or encoded text.

Cognizant Security Office (CSO) The Defense Contract Administration's regional office, having jurisdiction over the geographical area of various facilities. For example, a defense industry located in San Fernando, California, would find its CSO in Los Angeles.

COIN Post–World War II term from the US Air Force meaning *counterinsurgency*.

cold approach A method of approaching a possible defector from the opposition and soliciting that very defection. Say, for example, a suspected KGB officer in the Soviet embassy at Tokyo showed all the signs of being dissatisfied with his life. His wife was a shrew, he liked the way

Western women look and act (not all defections were for ideological reasons), he had his eye on a new Datsun 240Z, his KGB boss chewed him out yesterday for a botched job. . . . If word got back to US intelligence via neutral channels that the KGB man was "considering," an officer may have approached him cold and offered cash (well worth it for his information) as well as security with a new I.D. in the West and a safe removal from the host country where all this was taking place. The latter was a real plus, as the KGB had engaged in shoot-outs, not to mention rough work, to get its people back.

cold warrior A sometimes pejorative term used to describe the older agents and officers that were products of the Cold War of the 1950s and 1960s. Often very paranoid about all Soviet intentions, they viewed the USSR as having absolutely no redeeming value other than that of a nuclear-testing site.

collate To critically compare two or more items or documents concerning the same general subject. Collation is normally accomplished in the processing phase of the intelligence cycle.

collection agency Any individual, organization or unit that has access to sources of information and has the capability of collecting from them.

collection plan A logical plan for determining indications from intelligence requirements and translating them into orders and requests for specific information.

color-coded doors Within the CIA, National Security Agency and other agencies, certain doors are painted various colors to designate who has access. The color will correspond to the security clearance and need-to-know of the employee.

columnar coordinate In cryptography, a symbol normally at the top of a matrix identifying a specific column of cells.

columnar transposition In cryptography, transposition in which the transcription is always by columns or vertical transcription.

combat intelligence The knowledge of the enemy, weather and geographical features required by a commander in planning and conducting combat operations.

COMINT *See* communications intelligence.

commercial code Sometimes called *private code;* used originally to save on intercontinental cable charges, later on to ward off industrial espionage. It is still available to cable users by private suppliers of code.

commercial division That unit within an intelligence service charged with developing a business or commercial cover for an agency or officer not operating out of an embassy. A singleton, for example, would use a commercial cover. Thus, a book salesman for a US publisher, having western Europe as his territory, could move fairly easily. Sometimes a bona fide US firm will allow use of its name and offices as cover for an officer.

commercial drop   Similar to a dead drop but using a viable and ongoing business as the intermediary.

Committee for Overhead Reconnaissance (COMOR)   A formal subcommittee of the US Intelligence Board formed in 1960 as a result of the U2 program. It was responsible for development and operations of overhead recon.

Common Knowledge, Operation   Nickname given the Inchon invasion by the press corps stationed in Tokyo during 1950. In this prime example of compromise, the alleged lack of invasion security didn't seem to hurt. *See* compromise.

communications analysis   The analysis of communications signals and the results of that analysis.

communications intelligence (COMINT)   Technical and intelligence information derived from foreign communications by other than the intended recipient.

communications, office of   A generic term for any facility handling communications; common in military as well as civilian usage.

communications security (COMSEC)   COMSEC is the protection resulting from all measures designed to deny unauthorized personnel information of value, which might be derived from the possession and study of telecommunications, or to mislead unauthorized persons in their interpretations of the results of such possession and study. So, beyond the protection of the privacy of the communication, it might involve countermeasures to plant misleading information over what a hostile force might consider a good tap.

communications security account   An activity responsible for maintaining custody and control of communications security material, normally identified by an assigned account number. Also known as *COMSEC account* and *ComSec account*.

communications security aids   All communications security material, other than equipment or devices, that performs or assists in the performance of cryptographic functions, or relates to associated functions and equipment, and is required in the production, operation and maintenance of cryptosystems and components thereof.

communications security analysis   The study of communications to determine the degree of cryptosecurity, transmission security and emission security afforded those communications.

Communications Security Central Office of Record   The primary unit charged with maintaining control over all accountable cryptomaterial charged to the Department of the Army.

Communications Security Command Issuing Office   An organization that distributes cryptomaterial within an overseas command and acts as an intermediate officer of record for all cryptomaterial used within that command.

communications security custodian (formerly called "cryptocustodian")   The individual designated by proper authority to be responsible for the receipt, transfer, accounting, safeguarding and destruction of COMSEC material.

communications security distribution authority A unit established by the responsible commander to provide communications security logistic support as necessary and appropriate to designated organizations.

communications security field army issuing office An organization organic to a field army capable of providing communications security logistic support to that army.

communications security information All information concerning communications security and all communications security material. *See also* cryptoinformation.

communications security logistics The logistics of the requirements of computation, acquisition, cataloging, distribution, storage, management, overhaul, and disposal of communication security equipment, aids and unique repair parts; cryptoaccounting of communications security equipment and aids; maintenance engineering; management and support of communications security equipment; technical assistance; and new equipment introduction. That is the "book" definition, and it's a mouthful. *Logistics* is the key word.

communications security material control system The specific system through which certain communications security material (particularly all keying material used to protect classified information) is distributed to users and through which safeguards are maintained.

communications security office of record and issue An office authorized to distribute and be responsible for accounting control of cryptomaterial.

communications security regional issuing office Activities established within the continental United States (CONUS) to provide communications security logistic support to specified regions within the army worldwide.

communications security surveillance The systematic examination of telecommunications to determine the adequacy of communications security measures, to identify communications security deficiencies, to provide data from which to predict the effectiveness of proposed communications security measures and to confirm the adequacy of such measures after implementation.

communications security system The complete collection of all factors that, taken together, are intended to provide communications security for a specific telecommunications system. This includes cryptographic transmission, emission and physical security features.

communist action organization Any organization in the United States whose charter, direction and purpose are determined by the State Department to be controlled by a foreign communist power. This classification *does not* include a diplomatic representative or UN mission accredited by the State Department.

communist front organization Any organization, other than a communist action organization as defined above, which is substantially controlled, directed or dominated by a communist action organization, and is primarily operated for the purpose of giving aid and support to a communist action organization, a communist government or the communist movement.

Company, the   The CIA. The term is also heard in reference to other organizations, such as Air America, Gibraltar Steamship Line and so on. Insiders will also refer to the CIA as the "Tea and Biscuit Company."

compartmentation   In unconventional warfare, the division of an organization or activity into functional segments or cells to restrict communication between them and prevent knowledge of the identity or activities of other segments except on a need-to-know basis. While this definition is right out of the book for UW, it would also apply to any intelligence-gathering operation. In cryptography, compartmentation is the restricting of certain variables in crypto to certain other users, thus limiting access to the protected information to prevent compromise of an adverse nature.

compromise   A loss of security resulting from exposure of classified information to an unauthorized individual by disclosure of documents or material or by an officer's or agent's cover being blown. Facilities, assets and idigenous sources are subject to compromise as well. *Compromise* is a terrible word to the intelligence professional!

CONFIDENTIAL   The designation applied to information and material, the unauthorized disclosure of which could reasonably be expected to cause damage to national security. Examples of damage include the compromise of information that indicates strength of ground, air and naval forces in the United States, as well as overseas areas; and disclosure of technical information used for training, maintenance, etc.

confidential informant   Usually an unpaid informant who provides inside information to an intelligence officer. Motivation can be anything, including disgust, revenge, honor, anticommunism, morality, etc.

conjecture compromise   Suspected compromise, as when a classified document is lost.

contact division   A former CIA division that contacted scientists, journalists, students and others in order to brief and debrief them on their trips to the Soviet Union and Eastern Bloc countries.

contingency fund   A substantial fund (some say up to $50 million) kept by director of Central Intelligence for unexpected supersecret operations that demand funding beyond the allocated, and classified, budget amount.

Continuity of Operations Plan   A well-thought-out plan to counter any interruptions an operational plan might encounter—compromised agents, killed agents, or botched moves physically—or to be accomplished with the usage of two (or more) isolated "bunkers" able to accommodate dozens to hundreds of US employees that would allow the US government to function in the event of a catastrophic attack. The first of these was under the Greenbriar Hotel in West Virginia. Commissioned by the Eisenhower administration and using a cover construction firm called Forsythe Associates, the site in a thick-walled fortress, was capable of holding the entire US Congress. Code-named PROJECT GREEK ISLAND, this facility, to the best of my knowledge, was activated only once, during the 1962

Cuban missile crisis. It was a secret facility until 1992 when the *Washington Post* revealed it.

contour flying   Low-level flying, literally flying over the contour of the ground. Contour flying is used for covert insertion of paramilitary troops, reconnaissance or airborne insertion into a target area, primarily to avoid radar or other detection devices.

contract agent   A one-time hire agent used for a specific task, after which he is free to solicit other employment; or a contract officer. Counterinsurgency experts, for example, are hired as advisors by the Agency.

control   The point in a chain of command responsible for an operation or part of an operation. The amount of authority varies.

controlled agent   An agent who is under direct control of intelligence officers and who is supported by the funds he receives for his work.

controlling authority   The organization responsible for directing the establishment and operation of a cryptonet. When the cryptonet utilizes cryptoequipment embodying electronic keying principles, the controlling authority is also responsible for generation and distribution of cryptographic key variables.

COPPER GREEN   Alleged to be code name for harassment of Iraqi prisoners to elicit information under stress.

cordon and search A technique used in insurgency warfare or internal control operations to isolate a small population group or designated area (cordon) in order to permit a detailed search for personnel or materials.

COSMIC TOP SECRET The NATO TOP SECRET document designation, signifying the document is the property of NATO and that it is subject to special security control.

counterinsurgency The military, paramilitary, political, economic, psychological and civic actions taken by a government to defeat insurgency. A new term has cropped up recently: *internal defense development (ID/D)*. *See* US counterinsurgent forces.

counterintelligence That aspect of intelligence activity devoted to destroying the ability of enemy foreign agents to collect information. In addition to neutralizing the enemy's agents, it is charged with protecting information against espionage, individuals against subversion and materials against sabotage.

counterintelligence appraisal An evaluation of the enemy's intelligence, sabotage and subversive capabilities to determine the relative probability of the enemy putting those capabilities into action. Simply, knowing the enemy's strength.

counterintelligence check A limited inspection performed either during or after duty hours to determine compliance with established security policies and procedures.

counterintelligence inspection   An inspection performed to determine compliance with established security policies and procedures. The inspection may involve more brass and a deeper look at all security than a counterintelligence check.

counterintelligence plan   A systematic listing of all intelligence countermeasures to be carried out by a command, indicating the units and agencies responsible for the execution of each risk.

counterintelligence survey   A survey conducted to determine the security measures required to protect installations from possible sabotage, espionage, subversion and unauthorized disclosure of, or access to, classified defense information.

counterintelligence technical survey   A survey for the purpose of ascertaining whether offices, conference rooms, war rooms and other locations where classified information is disseminated are free of technical surveillance monitoring systems.

counterleak   Done to counter the damage done by the initial leak or simply to imply a conspiracy between the original leak and the person running with it: for example, a reporter, politician or adverse agency.

counterpart   The person to whom the advisor, as a matter of assigned duty, renders technical and operational advice and assistance. This is primarily a preinsurgency and ongoing insurgency term.

countersabotage   Action designed to destroy the effectiveness of foreign sabotage activities through the process of identifying, penetrating, manipulating, neutralizing or repressing individuals, groups or organizations conducting or capable of conducting such activities.

counterspy   A lay term for a mole, or penetration of the enemy's network or organization. If the spy is the sword, the counterspy is the shield.

countersubversion   Counterintelligence that is devoted to destroying the effectiveness of inimical subversive activities through deception, detection, identification, exploitation, penetration, manipulation and repression of groups, individuals and organizations capable of such activities.

country desk   The part of an intelligence agency responsible for a certain country. It may actually be one desk or dozens of desks.

Country Team   The senior in-country US coordinating and supervising body. Generally headed by the chief of the US diplomatic mission, usually an ambassador, and comprised of senior members of each department, agency or division of the armed forces, the Country Team was developed after World War II to coordinate US government agencies in a foreign country.

courier   A person authorized to hand-carry classified material.

cover   A false title and job description provided intelligence officers operating in foreign countries. The Soviet Union supplied press and commercial cover for a large number of its KGB officers. Most cover provided US intelligence officers is very light, and thus after a period of a year or so in a foreign country, officers are known to hostile intelligence services.

cover for action Some plausible activity to explain the lifestyle, friends and possessions of a deep cover officer in a foreign country. Cover for action is similar to *cover for status*, below.

cover for status A pseudolegitimate occupation accorded an officer in order to cover his presence in a foreign country.

cover name Similar to a code name except that it is usually a "working name"—that is, an alias used on a false I.D. to which an officer must become accustomed. *See* cover.

cover story Fictional explanation of an officer's mission; the officer's cited reason for being in a particular, possibly hostile, foreign country. This is where good cover backstopping comes into play, as any foreign country can check out the "visiting American's" credentials through its embassy in the United States.

coverage Protection against risk to the national security by the use of intelligence around the globe. Having one agent in a remote corner of the world constitutes CIA coverage of that corner.

covert Secret.

covert action *See* covert operations.

covert operations Operations planned and executed so as to conceal the identity of, or permit plausible denial by, the sponsor. Such operations differ from clandestine operations in that emphasis is placed on concealment of the identity of the sponsor rather than on concealment of the operation.

crateology A science, originally an art, for judging the contents of crates seen topside on Russian trawlers. A good crateologist can immediately discern a missile, parts or even a fighter being smuggled into a contested area. Developed during the Cuban missile crisis, crateology is now tradecraft.

crime shop A title Ernest Hemingway gave to his little group looking for German U-boats operating off Cuba during World War II. He was funded $500 a month by the US ambassador in Havana to seek out and report on U-boats by using his many "fishing buddies." Burdened with rumors of wild parties with cohorts, the funding was stopped despite at least one documented sighting. Hemingway wrote of this in *The Old Man and the Sea*.

cross targeting A result of intelligence analysis of one country's activities that produces information about another country's movements or targets, usually as a result of communication between the two countries.

CRYPTO Designation or marking that indicates classified operational keying material, requiring special consideration with respect to access, storage and handling.

cryptoaccount An account maintained by an authorized holder of cryptomaterial for which periodic accounting is required.

cryptoanalyze To solve encrypted messages *without access* to the decryption system; in other words, by deduction and analysis without using the key.

cryptoancillary equipment Equipment specifically designed to facilitate efficient or reliable operation of cryptoequipment but which does not perform any of the functions of cryptoequipment. It can also be equipment designed specifically to convert information to a form suitable for processing by cryptoequipment—anything from a digital printout to a printout from a matrix printer of a cheap computer.

cryptoboard A group of personnel charged with encrypting and decrypting messages and communications.

cryptocenter A compartment or room used by cryptographers or a cryptoboard.

cryptochannel Crypto aids and indicators constituting a basic unit in cryptographic communication.

cryptocommunication Any communication the intelligibility of which has been disguised by encryption.

cryptocompromise A compromise of cryptoinformation, or recovery of plaintext of encrypted messages by unauthorized persons through cryptanalytic methods.

cryptocorrespondence Letters, messages, memoranda, questionnaires, diagrams, reports and similar media that contain cryptoinformation (coded material) but that, unlike cryptomaterial, do not contain information.

cryptocustodian The individual designated by proper authority to be responsible for the custody, handling, safeguarding and destruction of cryptomaterial.

cryptodate The date that determines the specific key to be employed.

cryptodevice A device that contains no cryptoprinciple, but that may be used with appropriate keying material to simplify encryption and decryption (not to be confused with cryptoequipment).

cryptoequipment Any equipment employing a cryptoprinciple.

cryptofacility A facility used for the operation, maintenance, research, development, testing, evaluation and storage of registered cryptomaterial.

cryptogram Any communication in visible but secret and possibly garbled text.

cryptographer One who encrypts or decrypts enciphered messages.

cryptographic Of, pertaining to, or concerned with cryptography. Normally abbreviated as *crypto* and used as a prefix.

cryptography The art or science of the principles, means and methods for rendering plaintext or information unintelligible for all but the intended recipient and for reconverting to plaintext that which is received encrypted.

cryptoguard 1) An activity responsible for decrypting, encrypting in another cryptosystem and relaying telecommunications for activities that do not hold compatible cryptosystems. 2) An activity responsible for providing secure telecommunications services for other activities.

cryptoinformation Any information that would make a significant contribution to the cryptoanalytic solution of encrypted text or a cryptosystem.

cryptomaterial, nonregistered Cryptomaterial that is accountable to the office of record and issue only on initial receipt and final disposition unless additional control measures are prescribed for specific material.

cryptonet Two or more activities with a common cryptosystem and a means of intercommunication; in other words, a communications network using crypto.

cryptonym A word, number or a combination thereof used to identify an agent or informant in order to conceal his true identity. All correspondence to the field stations utilizes cryptonyms. For instance, Juan Mendoza would be given a cryptonym such as *Tiger-1*.

cryptooperating instructions Instructions prescribing the methods to be employed in the operation of a cryptographic system. This includes a description of the cryptographic system as well as the method of application of specific keys.

cryptoperiod   A specific time period during which a particular set of cryptovariables may be used.

cryptoprinciple   A deterministic logic by which information may be converted to an unintelligible form and reconverted to its original, intelligible form. In other words, the cryptoprinciple is used in code breaking and enciphering.

cryptoproduction equipment   Equipment and components thereof specifically designed for and used in the manufacture and associated testing of cryptovariables.

cryptorelated information   Classified or unclassified information or material associated with, but not significantly descriptive of, a cryptotechnique or process or a cryptosystem or equipment or its functions and capabilities. Such information is not marked *CRYPTO*, nor is it subject to the special safeguards required for classified cryptoinformation.

cryptoservice   A message, usually encrypted, transmitted between cryptocenters, requesting or supplying information regarding irregularities in encryption or decryption of messages.

cryptosystem, general   Basic method employing certain invariable elements to encrypt and decrypt.

Crystal Palace   A reference to NORAD Headquarters, under Cheyenne Mountain in Colorado. NORAD—North American Aerospace Defense Command.

CTC Counterterrorist Center. A CIA unit or subdivision.

Cube Slang for Cuban; especially agents of the opposition, Cuban intelligence, the Direccion Generale de Inteligencia (DGI).

custodian An industrial security term for an individual to whom classified material is assigned, and who is responsible for its protection in accordance with Department of Defense regulations and private industry.

cut outs An individual within an espionage network who enables other officers or agents to remain anonymous; an important element. Often, either a principal or lesser cut out is used, with the principal making hiring and firing decisions and protecting the network leader and the lesser simply acting as an intermediary.

damage assessment debriefing   A debriefing held after an operation has been blown or compromised to anticipate potential and future problems and thereby minimize damage.

danger signals   Prearranged signals or marks on walls, posts, etc., as a communication system between agents or officers to indicate that the opposition or active enemy is nearby, has been tipped off, or has the area under surveillance.

dangle operation   An operation in which something or someone of interest to an opposition intelligence service is intentionally put into the path of another agent in hopes that he will bite and consequently expose himself or blow his operation.

date break The date on which a change in cryptographic procedure concerning keys, codes, etc., takes place.

dated Not just old, but also compromised information. A defector observed to be feeding his new bosses compromised, or dated, intelligence is usually suspected of being a double agent.

dead babies False identification. To have a lot of dead babies in your pocket is to carry several phony I.D.s. The expression comes from the practice of using a birth certificate of a person who died as a child as a basis for a false I.D. In most record centers, birth and death certificates are not cross-filed.

dead drop A place or receptacle where messages between intelligence agents or officers can be left and picked up, thus obviating the need for direct contact. Dead drops range from the classic hollow oak tree to the not-so-classic Greyhound Bus station locker.

debriefing 1) The process whereby any military member or civilian employee of the Department of Defense, CIA or other intelligence-gathering agency who has possession of defense or official information, or other facts or data of a sensitive nature, is instructed in the safeguarding of such information, prior to passing from the operations control of an agency or an activity in the service of which the information was acquired. 2) The simple procedure of extracting facts and data from an employee concerning his last assignment or experience.

debriefing oath An oath during debriefing on a highly sensitive project to emphasize both an earlier commitment to silence and the requirements of classified information.

decipher To translate an enciphered message into text using a cipher method and not cryptoanalysis.

declassification The change in status of information from classified to unclassified when it no longer requires, in the interests of the national defense, any degree of protection against unauthorized disclosure. Not to be confused with *downgrading*.

declassification event The actual event that results in a project, materials, data, etc., being declassified or losing the need for further protection. In a declassification event all weapons and personnel concerned will be declassified.

declassify To cancel the security classification of an item of classified material regardless of previous classification.

decode To translate code into plaintext by means of a code book. Loosely synonymous with *decipher*.

decrypt To convert a cryptogram to plaintext by reversal of the encryption process. Not to be confused with cryptoanalyze.

deep cover A very thorough false identity, usually established by burrowing into the fabric of a hostile community for a number of years, possibly nine or more, before "coming alive," or surfacing, in an intelligence role. One usually severs all governmental contacts except pay (always forwarded, though well covered) and, on reactivation, discreetly performs intelligence activities. The Soviets used deep cover frequently.

defection in place   *See* agent in place.

Defense Advanced Research Projects Agency (DARPA)
A fifty-plus-year-old agency specializing in covert, risky and outside-the-box projects. From developing stimulants to keep soldiers aware, to shoes with the imprint on the sole of a human's bare foot to confuse locals as to who is operating in a given area, to a tiny camera designed to look like a small bird or insect and that actually flew.

defense condition (DEFCON)   Rating of defense readiness, from 1 through 5, with 5 being full-state readiness.

defense information   Official information that requires protection in the interests of national defense. It is not common knowledge and would be of intelligence value to an enemy or potential enemy in the planning or waging of war on the United States. The three categories of defense information, in descending order, are: TOP SECRET, SECRET and CONFIDENTIAL.

Defense Intelligence Agency (DIA)   An agency established by Robert McNamara in 1961 to control DoD intelligence resources and review activities of various service intelligence units.

delegated authority   That authority granted by an executive order for delegation of classification tasks. Also, for example, the chief of a division can delegate authority for approval of operational directives to a branch chief.

denied areas   In international espionage, it was usually the Iron Curtain countries; in industrial security, the off-limit areas containing classified matters or documents.

deputy director (DD)   The CIA has a director and four deputy directors, as follows: deputy director of operations; DD of science and technology; DD of intelligence; and DD of administration.

derivative classification   That classification resulting from, in connection with, or in response to existing material that is already classified. For example, a diagram of a harmless knob can become TOP SECRET when attached to a TOP SECRET missile.

desk   Slang for office or offices that comprise a section or interest in an intelligence agency; usually refers to a country (Israel desk) but can also refer to an ongoing project or operation.

destabilization   An attempt to destabilize a foreign country through covert action. The term was created by the media, credited to Daniel Schorr, yet ascribed to former CIA Director Richard Helms.

destruction procedures   Approved procedures for destroying classified documents by burning or other methods.

Deuxième Bureau   The French Intelligence Service. The term was used during the 1950s, but is now out of date.

devised facility   A false business run by the CIA as a cover for an operation or agent under commercial cover. Unlike a proprietary business, the devised facility conducts no actual commercial business.

Dial X   A highly classified internal communications system for a Polaris submarine.

digraph   Two letters used in a US agent's code name to indicate the country in which he is working. For example, the digraph for Vietnam is *TU*. Thus, a street whore working for the United States in Vietnam would be coded *TUWHORE*. Real names of agents are never used in communication.

Direccion Generale de Inteligencia (DGI)   Cuban intelligence. In the early days of DGI, after the Castro overthrow, DGI men were easy to spot due to their bulky "zoot suit" clothing, obvious .45 on the hip and small stature. Later, the KGB polished the DGI men, as well as its own personnel.

direction   *See* Appendix 3: The Intelligence Cycle.

Directorate A   A disinformation unit within the Soviet KGB.

Directorate of Operations   The CIA directorate currently responsible for all HUMINT operations.

Directorate of Plans   CIA directorate established in August 1952 as an organizational entity that included in one clandestine service the functions of secret intelligence collection, counterintelligence and covert action. It is known as the Directorate of Operations.

Directorate of Science and Technology   Sometimes called the Directorate of Dirty Tricks, this is the CIA office responsible for developing the working tools of tradecraft. This directorate applies scientific and psychological research to such projects as handling agents, building microphones, setting up bugging systems, disguising officers and designing gasses, night optics, voice alteration methods, etc.

Directorate V   The Soviet directorate within the KGB that specialized in wet work, or wet operations, also known as assassination. *See* wet work.

dirty, dirtied   Blown, exposed. An operation or an officer can be dirtied.

disaffection   Alienation or estrangement from those in authority; a lack of loyalty to the government or Constitution of the United States. Disaffection is not necessarily treason or sedition, but is close enough to cause concern.

disinformation   In Russian, *disinformatsiya;* untruths disseminated by placing misleading information in a friendly medium with hostile intentions. The Soviet Directorate A was responsible for planting communist disinformation, and the free press of the Western nations was more vulnerable than the media liked to admit.

disseminate To distribute classified material under continued control of the US government to persons having proper clearance and need to know. This could be from the CIA to the FBI, to the State Department, or to the White House.

distancing The technique of separation from someone or something. With an agent about to be compromised, an officer or agent handler might start to develop some latent cut outs or begin distancing in order to avoid being exposed or blown.

distribution codes Codes that indicate who is qualified to see or have access to specific classified items. A TOP SECRET clearance regarding the design of tactical tennis shoes will not, for example, permit clearance to a missile guidance section.

BUBERE Burn before reading. Some wag in a back room came up with this fictitious classification years ago.

EXDIS Exclusive dissemination; with a color-coded warning cover; dissemination might be under twenty people.

EARS ONLY A seemingly even more classified system beyond EYES ONLY. Highly classified data that cannot be put into print and communicated/discussed only in a special environment.

EYES ONLY   To be read by only one designated person; not to be copied, shown to others or passed on to any other activity. This is a stringent distribution code classification.

FGI   Foreign government information within; treat as sensitive matter.

LIMDIS   Limited dissemination or distribution.

NFIBONLY   Distribution for the National Foreign Intelligence Board only.

NOCONTRACT   A code designed to keep contractors and their personnel from accessing certain material, as in a defense-related matter. Some part of the blueprints, for example, would have to be seen by the contractor, but an addendum to the blueprints considered too sensitive would be coded NOCONTRACT.

NODIS   No distribution; originator controls document flow.

NOFORN   No foreigner. Indication that foreign nationals, even allies, are to be denied access to a document.

ORCON   Originator controlled. Information with this distribution code may *not* be passed on to a user agency without further clearance. Similar to NODIS.

PROPIN   Proprietary information, secured by copyright, patent or trademark, or of high value to the firm that possesses it. This is a defense-industry security term that turns up frequently.

Q CLEARANCE   Common, as these things go. Used for those with atomic or nuclear clearance: scientists, engineers, security, etc.

document   Any recorded information, regardless of physical form or characteristics, and exclusive of machinery, apparatus or equipment. The term includes, but is not restricted to, the following: all written material, whether handwritten, typed or printed; magnetic recordings; all photographic negatives, exposed or printed films, and still or motion pictures; all punched cards and tapes; and all reproductions of the foregoing.

DoD   Department of Defense.

Domestic Contacts Service   A group formed in 1946 under the control of the Central Intelligence Group (CIG) for utilizing domestic intelligence and contacting American businesses for overseas commercial cover.

Domestic Operations Division   A division of the CIA Clandestine Services that used to be headquartered in downtown Washington, D.C. Its exact mission is still a mystery.

dossier   A file of all known facts about a certain political or military figure; from the French, meaning "a bundle of papers." *Dossier* has a certain police-state ring to it and is considered a pejorative word in some Western government circles.

double agent   An agent working for two opposing agencies; he is loyal to one while betraying the other.

double back   To turn around, or reverse loyalties: "When the betrayed agency discovered the agent's duplicity, he was forced to double back." Often, the exposed double agent's only alternative is death, a most compelling reason for doubling back.

doublet   In cryptography, a diagraph consisting of a repeated letter.

down in Dixie   Israel; heard in Beirut, circa 1960, meaning "down south." The term is often used within intelligence, and the media have also gotten ahold of it.

downfield blocking   A common technique in all intelligence services of clearing an overt (or sometimes covert) act that might cause trouble or embarrassment with a friendly service. Considered an extension of professional courtesy, downfield blocking is not a standard procedure.

downgrade   To lower the classification of classified material in the interests of national defense. While to lower information classifications may sound peculiar, it serves a valuable end. When material is classified higher than it deserves to be, it is removed from use by those who have real need for it. Intelligence is useful only *if it is used*. Overclassification is almost as dangerous as underclassification, and some say it is more dangerous.

drop   *See* dead drop.

dummy agent   A fictitious agent invented for purposes of deception.

dummy message   A message, usually a total fabrication, sent for deception purposes only.

EARS ONLY   A distribution code designator meaning *information that cannot be put into print*. *See* distribution codes.

Eastern Construction Company   An offshoot of the Freedom Company, renamed the Eastern Construction Company in 1957. *See* Freedom Company for details.

economic action   The planned use of economic measures designed to influence the politics or actions of another state; for example, to impair the warmaking potential of a hostile power or to generate economic stability within a friendly power.

economic intelligence   Intelligence that deals with the extent and utilization of natural and human resources and in the industrial potential of nations.

economic warfare Intensified government direction of economic means of affecting foreign economies.

electromagnetic camouflage The use of electromagnetic shielding, absorption and/or enhancement techniques to minimize the possibility of detection and identification of troops, material, equipment or installations by hostile sensors employing radiated electromagnetic energy.

electromagnetic compatibility The ability of communications electronics equipment, subsystems and systems to operate in their intended operational environments without suffering or causing unacceptable degradation because of unintentional electromagnetic radiation or response.

electromagnetic cover and deception (EC&D) The suppression, control, alteration or simulation of electromagnetic radiations associated with friendly systems, equipment, devices or weapons components to deny an enemy knowledge of the location of combat elements or mislead him as to their capabilities and intentions. EC&D techniques include the use of emission control, electromagnetic camouflage and the manipulative/simulative electronic deception aspects of electronic countermeasures.

electromagnetic profile The compilation of identification, location and operational characteristics of equipment, devices or weapon-system components employing electromagnetic energy, which can reveal the deployment of combat forces, command and control centers or weapons and can thereby provide an enemy with knowledge of friendly capabilities and intentions.

electronic counter-countermeasures (ECCM) Electronic warfare (EW) involving actions taken to ensure our own effective use of radio communications and sensoring equipment despite hostile ECM.

electronic countermeasures (ECM) Action taken to deny enemy use of radio communication systems and sensors by means of jamming and electronic deception techniques.

electronic deception Military action taken to deceive the enemy through the use of imitative communications, deception, manipulative electronic deception and various radar deception techniques.

electronic intelligence (ELINT) Intelligence derived from the interception and analysis of hostile noncommunications emitters such as radar and emitters that are components of navigational systems.

electronic security (ELSEC) Protection resulting from all measures designed to deny a real or potential enemy information of value that could be derived from the interception and study of friendly noncommunication sensors such as radars and electrooptical systems.

electronic warfare (EW) Military action involving the use of electronic equipment to gain intelligence; to exploit, reduce or prevent an enemy's use of electronic equipment while taking action to ensure use of electronic equipment by friendly forces.

electronic warfare support measures (ESM) Actions taken to search for, intercept, locate and immediately identify radiated electromagnetic energy for immediate threat recognition. ESM provide a source of information required for immediate action involving ECM, ECCM (watch those initials) avoidance, targeting and other tactical employment of forces. That's the official definition. Put simply, support measures enable the commanders in the field to find out what the enemy is up to and where it is located.

elicitation The art of getting a foreign government official to provide important information during an apparently casual social conversation.

ELSUR Electronic surveillance.

emanations security The protection resulting from all measures designed to deny unauthorized persons information of value that might be derived from interception and analysis of compromising emanations from other than cryptoequipment and telecommunications systems.

emergency cryptosystem A cryptosystem designed to provide security of communications in a cryptonet when the systems normally used have been compromised or used up, until system replacements are distributed to all stations in the net.

empty vessel   A defector who has only selected information to give his new hosts. Usually, an empty vessel has been set up by his old masters who, knowing full well his potential for defection, have supplied him with false information. If his former employers *allowed* him to defect, they probably considered that he carried no important or timely information that would prove adverse to their cause. There is also the "dummy defection," wherein an agent fakes a defection to another country; his goal is to join and penetrate an opposition intelligence organization. Hours and months of debriefing are necessary to establish a defector's bona fides in order to determine whether he is, in fact, an empty vessel.

encipher   To convert plaintext into an unintelligible language by a cipher system, usually letter by letter.

enciphered code   A cryptosystem in which a cipher system is applied to encoded text.

encode   1) That section of a code book in which the plaintext equivalents of the code groups are in alphabetical, numerical or other systematic order. 2) To convert plaintext into unintelligible form by means of a code system.

encrypt   To convert plaintext into unintelligible form by means of a cryptosystem. The terms *encrypt, encipher* and *encode* are often used interchangeably.

encrypted text   Text encoded to convey either no message or a deceptive message to those who don't know the decryption system. For example, the above sentence, decrypted, means "Your pizza is ready."

escape and evasion (E&E)   The procedures and operations whereby military and civilian personnel are able to emerge from enemy-held or otherwise hostile areas to friendly control.

escape chit   A means of identification, normally made of cloth, upon which is printed, in the language of the area, a message promising a reward for assisting the bearer to safety. Replicas of the US and Allied flags are sometimes superimposed on the escape chit as well.

espionage   1) The art of spying. 2) The act of seeking information for one government that another government wishes to keep secret.

espionage notation   Notation required for application to all classified materials (except restricted matter), which is furnished to authorized persons (except the executive branch) to inform recipients of the federal prohibition against unauthorized disclosure.

espionage revolution   The practice, generally accepted among the major powers, of exchanging rather than executing captured spies. Concept is credited to New York attorney James Donovan in his defense of Rudolph Abel, a Soviet spy. Major powers realized it was expedient to maintain a reciprocal agents trade policy.

essential elements of information (EEI)   The critical items of information regarding the enemy and the environment that are required to make timely decisions.

evaluation   The step in the processing phase of the intelligence cycle in which an item of information is appraised in terms of credibility, reliability, pertinency and accuracy.

exchange commodity   A commodity given in lieu of cash or valuables for services rendered by an agent. It can be something of value, such as a ticket out of the country, but more often it is something that money alone can't buy, such as a US passport, new I.D., weapons or even a vote in the assembly of an emerging nation.

exclusion area   A restricted area containing a security interest or other matter that is of such a vital nature that access to the area, or proximity resulting from access, constitutes for all practical purposes access to the particular security interest or matter.

executive action   A term, popping up occasionally, that orders the "termination" of an important individual, particularly a friendly, who stands in the way of a sinister plot to take over the government.

executive order   An order with the force of law issued by the president by virtue of the authority vested in him by the Constitution or an act of Congress.

extraction The quick-as-possible removal/extraction of a target from a generally hostile environment. Stealth, quiet, efficient are the three main traits of an extraction.

EYES ONLY A distribution code designator meaning *to be read by only one designated person. See* distribution codes.

F

facility clearance   The security clearance granted by the Department of Defense to a plant, laboratory, office, college, university or commercial structure that deals in classified projects, contracts, etc. Clearance may be revoked by the cognizant security officer (CSO) for security deficiencies, and appeal is not authorized.

faith-based intelligence   Intelligence derived from a more analytical base of intelligence solely to bolster prejudicial-based data and interpretation. In other words, selective facts and data to bolster a closed mind.

false-flag operation   A project or operation sponsored by one government under the pretense that another government is the sponsor. For example, CIA officers might pretend to be KGB officers while employing foreign nationals to disrupt a meeting or stage a demonstration "for the good of the Party."

false-flag recruitment The act of recruiting an agent to participate in a false-flag operation. This recruit will unwittingly be serving the "wrong" side.

Family Jewels A list of controversial activities of the CIA from early 1962 to 1972 compiled by former CIA director William Colby. The list was ordered for Senator Frank Church's Senate Committee hearings on the CIA and is considered by many in the intelligence community to be an overzealous confession on the part of Colby.

Farm, the Camp Peary, the Williamsburg, Virginia, training base of the CIA, where potential CIA officers learn the tradecraft of espionage, covert actions, special operations, etc.

FE/Plans CIA designation for Far East Division, Plans Branch.

FGI A distribution code designator meaning *Foreign government information within; treat as sensitive matter. See* distribution codes.

field information report An information report written in the field (foreign country) and sent to headquarters for dissemination.

field of interest One or more categories of classified material that relate directly to the work assignment of an individual.

field project outline   An intelligence-operation report outlining funding requests.

field project renewal   An intelligence operation's annual request for funds.

filbert base   A general naval term used to describe the deception operation of setting up a dummy air or naval base, as on D day 1944, to lead an enemy to expect an attack from a false location. Such an operation would entail using rubber airplanes, landing craft, vehicles, etc.

finished intelligence   The end product of the intelligence cycle. Finished-intelligence reports are issued daily by all intelligence agencies. *See* Appendix 3: The Intelligence Cycle.

Firm, the   British jargon for the British Secret Intelligence Service (SIS).

fix the hole   A commonly used term when discussing the need to close gaps in an operation or to fulfill a need when a certain leak in equipment, intel or personnel is evident.

flap   A scandal or blow-up of some kind. A flap is the political and public fallout of a blown operation.

flaps and seals   The unit of science and technology at the CIA that specializes in the ability to open and close any sealed document, file, dossier or envelope without leaving evidence. This is a highly valued old world skill, and a traditional part of spy tradecraft.

FLASH   A high-priority coding put on certain cable traffic. With the FLASH designation, a cable can reach the chief of any division or any deputy director at Langley, Virginia (CIA headquarters), from any point in the world in less than seven minutes.

flash backstopping   *See* backstopping, flash.

flash roll   A thick roll of bills that might be flashed in front of a possible agent for recruitment. Often, the CIA will develop cover for the Drug Enforcement Agency. When the flash roll is used in such operations, it is often counterfeit money that is treated to turn yellow or red within a week or so in case it should get into the wrong hands.

fluttering   Being put on the lie box, or polygraph, for any reason at the CIA.

For Official Use Only   Marking used by the military to indicate sensitive information restricted in the public interest because widespread dissemination could unduly interfere with the efficient functioning of the government, violate a legal or moral obligation or result in injury to an innocent person.

For the President's Eyes Only   This label or warning is placed on documents of various classifications, mostly TOP SECRET, that are destined for the White House.

foreign classified information   Official information of a foreign government that that government has classified;

the United States has determined to require protection in the interests of national defense; and has been furnished to a US contractor in connection with a contract or other arrangement approved by the US government. The US government is obligated to protect foreign classified information pursuant to an agreement. The code *FGI* as discussed in distribution codes would apply here.

foreign classified material   Official material of a foreign government that is classified or that the US government has determined to require protection in the interests of national defense.

foreign government information   1) Information provided to the United States by a foreign government, an international organization of governments or any element thereof with the expectation, expressed or implied, that the information, the sources or both, are to be held in confidence. 2) Information produced by the United States pursuant to or as a result of a joint arrangement with a foreign government or an international organization of governments or an element thereof requiring that the information, the arrangement or both be held in confidence.

foreign intelligence   All intelligence collected by the US intelligence community outside the United States.

Foreign Intelligence Surveillance Court   A court set up in 1978 to review all applications for electronic surveillance of foreign agents and their governments by the US government. There are seven district judges.

foreign interest   Any foreign government or agency of a foreign government; any form of business enterprise organized under the laws of any country other than the United States or its possessions; any form of business enterprise organized or incorporated under the laws of the United States or controlled by a foreign government, firm, corporation or person. Included in this definition is any person, except for an immigrant alien, who is not a citizen or national of the United States.

foreign service reserve officer (FSRO)   The classification held by most CIA officers while holding posts at stations within US embassies. It is the State Department cover allowed for these officers.

formerly restricted data   Information that has been removed from the restricted data category by joint action of the Atomic Energy Commission (AEC) and Department of Defense under section 142d of the Atomic Energy Act of 1953. Formerly restricted data cannot be made available to regional or foreign defense units except as the Atomic Energy Act allows.

Freedom Company   A CIA commercial cover, or proprietary, set up in 1954 by Ed Lansdale to help establish the Diem family in office in Vietnam. This company also served as a vehicle to infiltrate friendly Filipinos into the Republic of Vietnam. The Freedom Company trained Diem's troops, organized, or tried to organize, veterans throughout the world into an anticommunist organization, and in general tried to help the Vietnamese form a more democratic government.

G

general cryptosystem   *See* cryptosystem, general.

"Gentlemen do not read each other's mail."   Secretary of State Henry Stimson's words when he closed the only cryptoanalytic section the United States had in 1929. His naive remark hangs over many an intelligence analyst's desk today.

Gibraltar Steamship Company   A CIA proprietary that operated in the Caribbean during the early 1960s. It was cover for several "affairs," one of which was the covert radio station that made pro-American broadcasts to the Cuban population.

GLAVLIT   Acronym for the Soviet Chief Administration for Safeguarding State Secrets in Print. This KGB entity was charged with censoring all printed matter—medical, educational, scientific and so on—within the USSR.

going undercover   In which a hostile agent seeks employment with the targeted agency, unit or project. The risks are so great it is seldom done. *See* insertion and/or placement.

go-no-go   The conditions necessary for an operation to commence. Only two variables apply: *go*, functioning properly, and *no-go*, functioning improperly. "Is it a go or a no-go situation?" Or, "What's the go-no-go status?"

good'ole boy circuit   The network of information passed on, favors returned, jobs offered and contacts opened that exists for certain individuals lucky enough to be included. US Army Special Forces retirees are one of the better circuits. Former FBI agents have an excellent circuit as well, and some elements of the US Marine Corps have an established circuit. The good'ole boy circuit is typically an elite unit whose members share a common bond of special operations, danger and secrets. There are civilian good'ole boy circuits as well. Each circuit has its own dues requirements for membership.

GPU   Second name, after CHEKA, given to the Soviet intelligence system.

graphic arts   Facilities and individuals engaged in performing any consultation service or the production of any component or end product that contributes to the reproduction of classified information.

gray mail   A relatively new defense ploy whereby an individual arrested for gunrunning, intrigue, paramilitary activities or any other activity inimical to the United States will claim that he will expose the CIA if prosecuted. Often, the arresting agency will be baffled and conjecture that he may be telling the truth. On the stand, the defendant will claim he was working for the CIA, which has now abandoned him, and will then play on the sympathies of a sometimes gullible jury.

gray propaganda   *See* propaganda.

green house   An apartment or house used as a brothel for the purpose of blackmailing or compromising a certain targeted patron. This patron could be anyone from a KGB officer to an unfriendly local politico.

ground resolution   The film recording of detail taken by a spy in the sky satellite. The resolution is so high that legible photographs of license plates from fifty miles up are common.

GRU (Glavnoe Razvedyvatelnoe Upravlenie)   Soviet General Intelligence Directorate of the General Staff of the Red Army. Founded by Leon Trotsky in 1920, GRU served mostly as a military intelligence service. In some countries, GRU was in charge of all Soviet operations, and the KGB had to cooperate with it. GRU's high-priority target was US high technology.

guerrilla net   The network of guerrilla support activities used for waging guerrilla warfare in a hostile area, including the psywar ops, logistics, weapons, training and sanitation available to operatives.

guerrilla warfare   Military and paramilitary operations conducted in enemy-held or hostile territory by irregular and predominantly indigenous forces.

Gulf Steamship Company   *See* Gibraltar Steamship Company.

gumshoe   A spy or detective. The term is now seldom used.

hand receipt   A document used to record acceptance of, and responsibility for, communications security material from a communications security custodian.

handwriting   A British term, similar to the US term *signature*, meaning the particular style of an agent or officer, and the mark of his skill or lack thereof. "The assassination had Locke-Smith's handwriting all over it."

hard returns   The bottom line; the measurable results of the time and money spent for intelligence-gathering efforts.

hard targets   High-priority, and usually high-security, intelligence objectives. Whether the hard target is a head of state or a nuclear plant, the objective will be difficult to achieve.

hardened container   A sturdy container used in shipping to provide security protection by preventing the accidental loss of contents and to facilitate the detection of any tampering with the container while it is in transit. Some examples of hardened containers are banded or wired boxes, wooden boxes and closed cargo transporters.

hard-wired   The use of concealed microphones. Prior to the development of wireless and miniaturized transmitters for covert monitoring, the standard procedure was to use concealed microphones.

hero projects   Those projects, operations or extractions that are considered by insiders *too* daunting with only the most skilled and knowledgeable able to pull it off. A hero project.

high-grade cryptosystem   A cryptosystem designed to provide long-lasting security by inherently resisting solution for a comparatively long period or indefinitely.

Hill, the   The Hill is the term used for the Los Alamos National Lab in New Mexico.

hobby shop   A common term used to denote a military test facility. Could be missiles, planes, technical support gear, etc.

homophones   In cryptography, a system of multiple substitutes for letters. For example, *B* could stand for 8, 45, 38 or 78. Often a meaningless number, called a *null*, will be inserted for the sake of confusion.

host country   A nation in which representatives or organizations of another state are present because of government invitation or international agreement. The term particularly refers to a nation receiving assistance relevant to its national security.

House 7   A CIA safe house in Saigon.

House on 42nd Street   A CIA training facility that was on 42nd Street in New York City.

human sources   This is the best source of intelligence, according to some; others call it the most unreliable. Known as *HUMINT*, or *human int*elligence. Usually, *human sources* refers to nothing more than a local agent counting trains or ships in port.

HUMINT   An acronym used to describe intelligence gathered by human sources. See above.

I

imagery interpretation (II) The recognition, identification and description of objects, activities and terrain represented on imagery.

imitative communication deception (ICD) The intrusion into the enemy's radio communication system, including voice as well as machine intrusion, by the imitation of radio traffic and radio procedures to confuse or deceive the enemy. ICD was used by Allied forces to guide an Eastern bloc plane into a crash landing on a West European nation's soil by imitating the voice of the East Berlin traffic controller.

immediate message A category for placement of communications that seriously affect the security of the US national defense or that of US allies, indicating precedence of delivery and transmission.

imprest fund   Usually the source for money advanced to an intelligence informant, foreign national or agent.

indicator   In cryptography, an element within the text that will provide a guide for quick decryption.

industrial defense   All nonmilitary measures to ensure the uninterrupted productive capability of vital industries and resources essential to the defense of the United States. These measures are designed to minimize destruction and to expedite recovery after any damage, whether from sabotage or overt attack.

industrial espionage   The clandestine gathering of business information from a competitor. Based on the desire to know what one's competition is doing in order to get a piece of his market, industrial espionage is relatively risk-free due to gaps in the law. Although the game becomes more dangerous when one is dealing with international cartels or groups, often the captured culprit faces nothing more than the loss of his job. Corporations are now beginning to realize what an internal plant can cost them. Research for which the invaded corporation has spent millions winds up in the hands of a competitor, who pays nothing more than the spy's salary.

industrial security   The security arrangements of the US government that relate to the protection of classified material that is in the hands of private industry in the United States as a result of defense-related contracts.

information In intelligence, unevaluated data of every description that, when processed, may produce intelligence. *See* intelligence cycle.

information, nondefense Information that does not require safeguarding in the interest of national defense.

information circular A US government communication sent to various agencies and thousands of security and law enforcement agencies and officials but not publicly released.

information pollution To "drown" in information. A burdensome obligation to collect more and more presented data, which is a major concern of analysts.

information security Any system of administrative policies and procedures for identifying, controlling and protecting from unauthorized disclosure information the protection of which is authorized by executive order or statute.

insurgency A revolt or insurrection against a constituted government. There are generally considered to be three levels of insurgency:

Phase 1 At this stage subversive activities may be merely a potential or incipient threat, or subversive incidents or activities may already occur with frequency. During this initial phase, rebels recruit personnel and develop and organize an insurgent apparatus for use in subsequent phases. Phase 1 involves no major outbreak of violence or uncontrollable insurgent activity.

Phase 2 This stage is reached when the subversive movement, having gained sufficient local or external support, initiates organized guerrilla warfare or related forms of violence against the established authority. Operations to hold terrain objectives and engage in conventional warfare are avoided.

Phase 3 This stage is reached when the insurgency becomes primarily a war of movement (mobile warfare) between organized forces of the insurgents and those of the established authority.

insurgent warfare A struggle between a constituted government and organized rebels, frequently supported from outside the country, but acting violently from within against the political, social, economic, military and civil vulnerabilities of the regime to bring about its destruction or overthrow. Such wars are distinguished from lesser insurgencies by the gravity of the threat to the government and by the insurgents' goal of eventual regional or national control.

intelligence The product of the collection, evaluation and interpretation of information.

intelligence annex A supporting document of an operation plan or order that provides detailed information on the enemy situation, assignment of tasks and intelligence administrative procedures.

intelligence appraisal An assessment of intelligence relating to a specific situation or condition with a view to determining the courses of action open to the enemy or potential enemy and the probable order of their adoption.

intelligence committee Any group designed to oversee the collection, analysis and dissemination of intelligence. Most often an unofficial (in an operations sense) group appointed by a president.

intelligence community *See* Appendix 4.

Intelligence Coordination and Exploitation Program (ICEX) An effort to penetrate the Viet Cong. The first phase of ICEX was to neutralize the Viet Cong by arresting the tax collectors and the military who were home on leave. Later, more direct action was taken. The cover name of this program was Phoenix, and later, Phung Hoang.

intelligence cycle The steps by which information is assembled, converted into intelligence and made available to users. The phases of the intelligence cycle are direction, collection, processing and dissemination. *See* Appendix 3: The Intelligence Cycle.

intelligence evaluation *See* Appendix 1.

intelligence interrogation Systematic effort to produce information by direct questioning of a person under control of the questioner.

intelligence journal A chronological log of intelligence activities covering a stated period, usually twenty-four hours.

intelligence, negative Intelligence denied an enemy. Negative intelligence consists of known facts an enemy has taken or compromised, but which good counterintelligence has rendered valueless.

intelligence officer The principal staff officer assigned to advise and assist the commander in carrying out his intelligence and counterintelligence responsibilities.

intelligence report (INTREP) A specific report of information, usually on a single item, made at any level of command in tactical operations and disseminated as rapidly as possible in keeping with the timeliness of the information.

intelligence requirement Any subject, general or specific, upon which there is a need for the collection of information or the production of intelligence.

intelligence, scientific Espionage, counterespionage and covert operations of a highly technical nature. Dealing in all sciences, the officers involved in scientific intelligence are far removed from the old-time agent or officer skilled in spy tradecraft and nothing more. Often spending years in training, the officers are able to converse on their given subject with any target, friendly or hostile. The officer must be able to pass as the scientist he may profess to be.

intelligence, strategic Gathering of information—economic, social, geographical, military, civic, etc.—that pertains to the intentions of hostile or potentially hostile nations. Strategic intelligence is a product of the global wars of this century. Not only does a country's intelligence service produce strategic intelligence, but think tanks, by government contract, participate as well.

intelligence summary (INTSUM) A brief summary of intelligence covering a period of time designated by the commander, usually six hours.

intelligence workbook A systematic arrangement by subject heading that aids in the sorting, evaluation and interpretation of information and in the preparation of intelligence reports.

internal attack The full range of measures taken by organized insurgents to bring about the internal destruction and overthrow of a constituted government.

internal control operation Those military and nonmilitary activities conducted by the security forces of a nation (military, paramilitary, etc.) to cope with violence and lawlessness. The distinction between internal control operations and internal defense tactical operations is basically one of scope. While tactical operations are directed primarily against armed insurgents, internal control operations also include nonmilitary activities which security forces may conduct in coping with unarmed subversives.

internal defense   The full range of measures taken by a government to protect its society from subversion, lawlessness and insurgency.

internal defense assistance operation   Any operation undertaken by the military, paramilitary, police or other security agency of an outside power to strengthen a host government politically, economically, psychosocially or militarily.

internal defense operation   Any operation conducted by an ally or a host country's security establishment, military, paramilitary, police or security organization directly against armed insurgents, their underground organization, support system, external sanctuary or outside supporting power.

internal development   Environmental improvement. The strengthening of the roots, functions and capabilities of government with the goal of internal independence and freedom from conditions fostering insurgency.

internal development assistance operation   Any organized actions undertaken by government or nongovernment agencies of an outside power to support a host government's internal development efforts.

internal development operation   Any direct operation undertaken by a host government or its allies to strengthen the host government politically, economically, socially or militarily.

internal security 1) The prevention of hostile acts against the United States, its resources, industries and institutions and the protection of life and property in the event of a domestic emergency by the employment of all measures in peace or war other than military defense (industrial security definition). 2) The state of law and order prevailing within a nation (military definition).

interpretation The act of determining the significance of information in relation to the current body of knowledge through analysis, integration and deduction.

inventory A procedure designed to verify accountability of classified material by comparing entries on the register to the document itself, entries on the record of destruction or a signed receipt.

invisible ink A tradecraft "must" in ancient times, invisible ink has since fallen by the wayside. Earlier communications with milk, sugar and water, lemon juice, and other fluids were replaced with blue vitriol (copper sulphate), lead nitrate and some chlorides in the twentieth century. Usually heat or a chemical reagent would bring to the surface the invisible message usually hidden between the lines of visible text. Countermeasures to the invisible message have become too efficient, and microdot has generally, but not entirely, replaced it. Enciphered and coded electronic communications are the modern counterparts of invisible ink.

irregular forces Armed individuals or groups who are not regular armed forces.

J / K

jamming   The action taken to deny or degrade the enemy's use of radio communication through deliberate radiation, reradiation or reflecting of radio energy.

Jedburg   The Office of Strategic Services (OSS) unit that operated in France during World War II.

JMWAVE   The CIA clandestine radio station that operated in Miami, Florida, from 1960 to 1969.

key intelligence requirements   These are provided each US intelligence agency by the National Security Council (NSC). Each agency in turn has certain key requirements that it must report to the NSC.

key list   A publication containing the key for a cryptosystem in a given cryptoperiod.

key symbol In psychological operations, a simple, suggestive, repetitive element (rhythm, sign, color, etc.) that has an immediate impact on a target audience and that creates a favorable environment for the acceptance of a psychological theme.

key words Words that codebreakers look for within an intercepted transmission as indicators of a message with intelligence value.

keying material The cryptomaterial needed to arrange codes on the cryptoequipment or the material used directly in the encryption and decryption process; also, cryptomaterial that supplies sequences or messages used for command and control or authentication of a command or that can be used directly in their transmissions.

KGB *See* Komitet Gosudarstvennoe Bezopasnosti.

King's Secret An intelligence organization set up in 1740 by Louis XV of France, designed to circumvent established ministerial goals of the kingdom (i.e., covert ops) while giving lip service to official French policy.

Knight Former CIA director William Colby's code name when he headed the Phoenix program. *See* Intelligence Coordination and Exploitation Program (ICEX).

Komitet Gosudarstvennoe Bezopasnosti (KGB) The name of the Soviet Directorate of Intelligence.

Kremlinologist One charged with the study of all things pertaining to the Kremlin, Moscow and the Soviet Union in general.

L

L pill The lethal gray, red-banded cyanide capsule available to any operative who prefers death to the unbearable torture he believes would be the result of capture. Such an operative is not too different from the old cavalryman who saved the last bullet for himself.

lamplighters British term for support service personnel for operations; those responsible for transportation, manning surveillance posts, running safehouses, etc.

Lavon affair A major espionage scandal in Israel in 1950. Secret agents for Israel were ordered to blow up and sabotage American buildings in Cairo and Alexandria in an effort to sabotage American/Egyptian relations. The agents failed, through bungling and because one of them was a double agent for the Egyptian intelligence service, the Moukhabarat-el Kharbeya. Pinhas Lavon, defense minister of Israel, was blamed. He denied responsibility and maintained that Israeli military intelligence had been acting without authority. When an official hearing was unable to fix blame, David Ben-Gurion set up a new commission, which absolved Lavon but did not fix blame. Moshe Dayan was accused of conspiring against Lavon, but nothing was proved, and the scandal ended without resolution in 1961.

leak As it implies, an unauthorized release, or passing-on, of information to a contact or source that is sometimes accidental or, mostly, deliberate.

leaker A benevolent term to describe a whistle-blower. Often viewed by the public as beneficial and from within as a *#!#! Sometimes a fink.

leakman A journalist or editor considered friendly to the intelligence community. Information more valuable if released than held is passed on to leakmen for public exposure. Often, a nonleakman thinks that by publishing a story he is exposing the agency while, in fact, he is being used by the agency to further its cause somewhere in the world.

legals and illegals A systematic method of espionage that was carried on by the Soviet Union. A *legal* was an espionage agent or officer with legitimate cover: an embassy or trade mission, for example. The *illegal* had to slip into a target country and there set up a small business, develop a false passport and birth certificate, cover, etc. Unlike a legal, he had freedom of movement, but could not claim diplomatic immunity if caught. Worse, he could be ignored or disavowed by those who sent him. Both KGB and GRU used these systems extensively.

legend   A fictional operational plan for a cover, or the cover itself; a false biography. A legend may be a false trail completed to cover a false or notional biography.

letterbox   *See* dead drop. In French, *boite aux lettres*.

lexpionage   The act of finding new words pertaining to espionage matters often made necessary to communicate in brief and efficiently.

live drop   A person who unwittingly carries or communicates some message or device between an agent handler and an agent or case officer and his superior. A librarian may give so-and-so a book (containing a message) or a butcher may deliver a pound of liver to "my wife." Unbeknownst to the butcher, the weight of the meat is a prearranged code conveying a message to another party. Live drops appear innocuous, but are meaningful to those who send and receive them.

lodgment   A footfold gained within an enemy's espionage apparatus; it could be the recent defection of a hostile agent in a spy network.

long title   The full name or title assigned to a classified object, publication, item, piece of equipment or device. *See* short title.

loss   Classified material that is out of the control of its custodian or cannot be located.

low-grade cryptosystem   A system designed to provide temporary security, such as a combat or operational code.

low-intensity operations   A British term for guerrilla or counterguerrilla warfare.

main enemy Soviet term for the United States. It is used throughout most literature intended for in-house circulation and is used casually in discussions of the United States.

manipulative communications cover Those measures taken to alter or conceal the characteristics of communications so as to deny an enemy or potential enemy the means of identifying such communications.

manipulative communications deception The alteration or simulation of friendly telecommunications for the purpose of deception.

manipulative electronic deception The use of friendly radio and sensor equipment to mislead a foreign nation or enemy by presenting false indications for their analysis and to cover the real intentions of friendly forces.

marking   Placement of security classifications and required security notations on classified material.

material   In the field of security, any document, product or substance on or in which information may be recorded or embodied.

material control station   An activity or unit designated to record, receive, dispatch and maintain accountability of classified material *other than documents*.

message indicator   A group of symbols usually placed at the beginning of the text of an encrypted message or transmission that identifies or governs the arrangement of crypto-variables applicable to the message or transmission.

Miami   Home of a large international intelligence community, involving the CIA, FBI, Cuban intelligence, etc. The Caribbean is a hot spot of drugs, sex, guns, coups and revolution, and Miami is a good tap into the area. Exile groups are plentiful.

microdots   The technical ability to reduce a page of data to the size of a dot over an *i*. This information can then be hidden in a routine typed letter; special equipment is then necessary to enlarge the dot to retrieve the information. Microdots are a modern counterpart of invisible ink.

mighty Wurlitzer   A system or method of inserting a "news" notice in a small or cooperative newspaper, in hopes that paper after paper, and eventually the wire services, would pick up this item of black information and disseminate it around the world. The supposed source, or originating paper, is forgotten as the planted story works its way to the front pages of the world's major papers. Used at one time by the CIA in Italy.

Military Intelligence 5 (MI5)   A British security service roughly equivalent to the FBI; often incorrectly called "M one five." Its arrest powers are enforced by the Special Branch of Scotland Yard. MI5's major functions are investigation, file-keeping, surveillance and deciding on the timeliness of arrest.

Military Intelligence 6 (MI6)   A British secret service responsible for foreign espionage. MI6 resembles the CIA as both are active in spy and counterspy activities. MI6 has a questionable past, with events ranging from capture of its operatives by German counterspies in World War II to the treacherous deeds of turncoat Kim Philby; but the professional way MI6 handled Soviet defector Oleg Penkovskiy redeemed it, and eventually MI6 cleared itself of the old charges that it had been penetrated.

mil-slang   Just that, slang of a military nature as opposed to civilian intelligence agencies. Friendly fire, snafu (situation normal all fouled up), etc.

mind-set   A mental attitude or position, often used pejoratively in reference to the biases of an individual who has been spoon-fed erroneous information.

mission support site (MSS)   In unconventional warfare, a relatively secure site utilized by a force as a temporary support site or stopover point during the conduct of operations.

mole The opposing faction's insert, or penetration, into an intelligence apparatus. Well-trained false defectors are a danger, and thus any defector's bona fides are carefully checked. Some interrogations can take up to three years. The real fear is not so much what a mole can glean from one's system as what false information, or disinformation, he can plant.

monoalphabetic Using one, and only one, cipher alphabet, as in a code system, as opposed to *polyalphabetic*.

monster rally The technique, selectively used by the CIA, of inundating an area with free tickets to an opposition cultural rally or political affair. A ticket handout promising "all you can eat and drink" might draw huge crowds of Indonesians at a Soviet technology rally originally set up for a certain business community. With the possibility of a riot entailed in crowds being turned away, no one is interested in hearing the target's excuse that false tickets were disbursed by the opposition, and the reputation of the targeted party will be spoiled. A monster rally in Japan once promised "lots of free Chinese food" at a Chinese Communist Exposition. Over 18,000 people turned out for an affair originally calling for 400 people.

Moscow Center The KGB's headquarters in Moscow.

Mossad le Aliyah Beth (Mossad) The main unit of Israeli intelligence. Mossad is *institution* in Hebrew; the full name means *Central Institution for Intelligence and Special Assignments* (or *Services*). Ranked by some experts among the top six or seven intelligence-gathering in the world, its interests remain relatively provincial (generally interests of other pro-Western nations).

Most Secret The former British version of the US TOP SECRET. The term may have been grammatically correct, but the UK dropped it in favor of TOP SECRET during World War II.

Moukhabarat-el-Amma The Egyptian presidential secret service.

Moukhabarat-el-Kharbeya The Egyptian military intelligence.

Mukhabart *or* **Moukhabarat** General term in Arabic countries for the intelligence service. It means, loosely, *listening post*.

MVD Name given to the Soviet intelligence service in its fifth purge, in 1946; later called the KGB.

N

naked Exposed, as of an agent or officer: "The Soviets know him, he's naked."

name trace A cooperative computer check by various intelligence agencies to ferret out a certain name and all information connected with it, including history, associates, work, AKAs and all other references contained in the computer systems.

nap-of-the-earth flight A flight as close to the earth's surface as vegetation or obstacles will permit while generally following the contours of the land. The pilot will maintain a general axis of movement within his preplanned air corridor. A nap-of-the-earth flight is often used in covert operations.

national foreign intelligence Intelligence about a foreign power that responds to the needs of the president,

National Security Council and others involved in the formulation and execution of national security and foreign or economic policy of the United States.

national intelligence   The intelligence necessary to form national security policy.

National Intelligence Estimate   A report put out on a regular basis by the Office of National Estimates that tries to reconcile the various reports coming in from other agencies in order to offer the president a consensus.

national intelligence officers (NIO)   Intelligence officers responsible for collection and production in designated fields. Senior NIOs report directly to Central Intelligence.

National Intelligence Programs Evaluations (NIPE) NIPE was set up by John McCone in 1963 as an evaluative program within the CIA for the national intelligence community.

National Intelligence Situation Report (NISitRep)   A report issued at frequent intervals to the director of Central Intelligence during any major crisis.

National Photo Interpretation Center (NPIC)   Established in 1961 as a result of the rapidly expanding U2 program, the nucleus of NPIC came from the CIA Directorate for Intelligence. It was staffed by CIA and military personnel. NPIC was a part of the Directorate for Intelligence until 1973, when it became integrated into the CIA's Directorate for Science and Technology (DS&T).

national security   A collective term covering both the national defense and the foreign relations of the United States.

National Security Act of 1947   The act that established the Central Intelligence Agency.

National Security Agency (NSA)   The major code-breaking agency for the United States. Established in 1952, NSA's mission is communications surveillance. It is the largest of US intelligence services and, by some accounts, the most efficient. It is certainly the least known (NSA is also said to stand for "Never Say Anything").

National Security Council (NSC)   The NSC is presided over by the US president and advises him on matters regarding national security by integrating all data regarding domestic, foreign and military affairs.

National Security Organization   Organization for overall national security under the president of the United States as commander in chief. It consists of the National Security Council, the Office of Emergency Planning, the CIA and the Department of Defense.

national wars of liberation   A communist euphemism for insurgency that was used to disarm Western critics.

NATO classified information   All classified information—military, political and economic—circulated within and by NATO, whether such information originates in the organization itself or is received from member nations or from other international organizations.

need to know Criterion by which one gets to see or handle classified material. SECRET or TOP SECRET clearance is not enough; one must have the *need to know*. This determination is made by the possessor of classified material, the custodian.

negative intelligence *See* intelligence, negative.

network A ring of spies who share a common goal, leader, target or enemy. The lowest level of ring is a cell. It contains experts in communications, explosives, photography, electronics, etc., and functions smoothly when connected by live and dead drops and couriers and compartmented by cut outs. Once penetrated, a spy ring is usually easy to disassemble. *See also* guerrilla net

NKVD Name of the Soviet intelligence service from 1934 to 1946; later called the KGB.

NOC Pronounced as "knock," is an acronym for "nonofficial cover." Primarily a CIA term used where one is operating without cover of diplomatic protection or US government employment. An example would be a CIA linguist in the Serbian embassy acting as a spook to collect evidence. Remember, just because one is an employee of the CIA does not mean he "works" the enemy; as a CIA employee, he may be anything but a field agent.

NOFORN A distribution code designator meaning *no foreign distribution*. *See* distribution codes.

nondefense information *See* information, nondefense.

nonregistered cryptomaterial Cryptomaterial that is accountable to the office of record and issue only on initial receipt and final disposition, unless additional control measures are prescribed for specific material.

notional Fictional. A fictional business, cover, name, etc. A notional business would be used as cover by a singleton or case officer where a commercial cover is necessary.

notional agent A fictional agent used by an intelligence organization for deception; a nonexistent person. Sometimes called a *dummy agent*, it is used often in deception operations to throw off the enemy.

Nuclear Weapons Security Program A Department of Defense program for the limited number of contractors involved in nuclear-weapons security. This program identifies certain positions categorized as CRITICAL or CONTROLLED, depending upon the degree of involvement with nuclear weapons. All personnel in CRITICAL or CONTROLLED positions must have a security clearance commensurate with the security classification of information required by their duties. Specific procedures are set forth separately in appropriate contractual agreements.

null A symbol used in cryptography with no decoding significance, used to confuse enemy cryptographers. It may have deceptive meanings to the enemy.

numbered document Any document numbered for administrative record-keeping purposes only, often confused with registered matter.

O

Ochrana   Secret police of the Russian tsar until the 1917 revolution; literally, *guard* in Russian. The Ochrana was replaced with the CHEKA, a much more brutal institution now called the KGB.

Office of Policy Coordination   The first covert-action unit of the CIA, responsible for covert action abroad.

office of record   1) An office designated to maintain records for specified operations. 2) An agency charged with maintaining the ultimate accounting records for registered publications.

Office of Special Operations (OSO)   Early Central Intelligence division. It was formed from the Office of Strategic Services as part of the newly formed Central Intelligence Group.

Office of Strategic Services (OSS)   The primary US intelligence and special operations unit during World War II. Not having an overall intelligence unit at the beginning of the war, President Roosevelt appointed William Donovan to head the OSS. Its World War II strength of 13,000 penetrated all of the world's hot spots and then some. When the war was over, President Truman disbanded the OSS, but out of these beginnings grew the CIA.

official information   Any information that is owned by, produced by or subject to the control of the US government.

offline cryptooperation   Encryption or decryption performed as a self-contained operation—distinct from the transmission of the encrypted text—by hand or machine, but not electrically connected to a signal line. *See* online cryptooperation.

OGPU   The name for Soviet intelligence, later the NKVD and KGB, for the years 1923 through 1934.

online cryptooperation   The use of cryptoequipment that is directly connected to a signal line, making encryption and transmission, or reception and decryption, or both together, a single, continuous process.

one-part code   A code for which a single code book serves for both encryption and decryption.

one-time code   Another name for the one-time pad.

one-time cryptosystem 1) A cryptosystem employing a one-time-use key. 2) A cryptosystem in which a cipher alphabet is used only once.

one-time pad A pad with a one-time-use key printed on each page, designed to permit the destruction of each page as soon as it is used. An agent in the field may have a pad the size of a postage stamp. Sometimes the pads are called "one-time Gammas."

one-time system A system of encipherment in which a nonrepeating key is used.

one-time tape A tape used in the keying element in a one-time cryptosystem.

open code A cryptographic system using external text, which has an external meaning but disguised hidden meaning.

OPERATION FIREWALL FAA or FBI and pentagon joint response to terrorist attack. If done in time, all points of entry would be secured to seek a target previously described and now known.

Operation Penis Envy According to reliable sources, a couple of officers attached to a CIA station in an Eastern bloc country dropped, near Soviet military installations, official-looking boxes with US markings from a plane. In the boxes were thousands of oversize condoms. The hope was that the Russian soldier who found them would wonder what kind of soldier the United States had.

operational climate Overall operating environment of agents, contacts, etc. The term refers to the political, social, economic, security and other aspects of the area.

operational desk The headquarters desk of each country in a branch of a CIA division.

operational expenses Monies allowed by an agency for procurement of potential agents, minor bribes, ticket fixing and, in general, hidden funds that would allow an intelligence officer or station to operate without having to itemize every expenditure to the Office of Management and Budget.

operational independence The delegation of certain (and limited) operational decision making to field agents to enhance response time and develop initiative, all with the goal of acquiring information.

operational intelligence Information required to conduct intelligence operations in a given country.

operational progress report A monthly progress report on a specific intelligence operation.

operations The action end of intelligence, behind the collection, analysis and disbursement of information. An operation could either produce information or be a direct result of information acquired through intelligence.

Operations Advisory Group (OAG) Formed from the 40 Committee (an intelligence advisory committee of selected individuals) and renamed by President Ford, it is a part of the National Security Council.

operations code   A code capable of being used for general communications. It is composed largely, though not exclusively, of single words and phrases.

Operations Coordinating Board (OCB)   A board set up by the National Security Council to oversee and coordinate the common purposes of overseas operations and projects of the various agencies.

operations security (OPSEC)   Actions taken to deny the enemy information concerning preplanned, ongoing and completed operations.

operations security officer   That officer responsible for security on and off a specific operation, project or undertaking.

opposition   The enemy, in the trade jargon.

order of battle (OB)   One of the most prized chess pieces of a spy, an OB consists of the enemy's basic information on ground-forces unit formation and provides all pertinent order-of-battle information. An OB is usually put together through prisoner interrogation, captured documents and intelligence gathering. Sometimes an agent or spy can come into possession of the complete data all at once.

original classification   An initial determination that particular information requires, in the interest of national security, protection against unauthorized disclosure, together with a classification designation signifying the level of protection required.

original classification authority   The authority required to independently classify any type of material. For the TOP SECRET classification authority, one has to fit the criteria specified in the most recent executive order. *See* classification authority.

originator   The commander or executive by whose authority an item of information is created and disseminated.

other intelligence requirements (OIR)   Items of information of secondary importance to essential elements of information (EEI) regarding the enemy and environment, which may affect the accomplishment of a mission.

outside officers   CIA officers in a given country who are located outside of the embassy.

overclassification   The overclassification of classified matter can be as dangerous as underclassification. Intelligence is totally useless unless it is used. To overclassify a document and thus deny someone in the command access to information he needs to perform his duty is to defeat the purpose of intelligence.

overt   Open; without attempt to conceal, as an "overt employee" for an intelligence service. "William Casey is an overt employee."

P / Q

Pacific Corporation A CIA holding company, alleged to have over 20,000 employees.

PACT Project Advancement of Coding Techniques; abandoned code-improvement project.

paper mills A generally negative term used to describe individuals who often turn up on an intelligence agency's doorstep offering to sell "explosive" or "sensitive" documents. "Damn, here comes that paper mill Juan again."

paramilitary Military forces that are distinct from the regular armed forces of any country but which resemble them in organization, equipment, training or mission.

paramilitary operation A military undertaking by a paramilitary force.

passport code The code used by some missions or embassies for minor administrative details.

pattern analysis The technique of analyzing and correlating a series of enemy events over a period of time and predicting future enemy trends, activities and courses of action.

penetration An insertion of an enemy spy within an intelligence organization.

perfect spy It has been said that the perfect spy would have a great deal of difficulty in catching a headwaiter's attention.

periodic intelligence report (PERINTREP) An intelligence summary covering a longer period of time than the standard six-hour intelligence summary.

permutation table A table designed for the systematic construction of code groups. It may also be used to correct garbles in groups of code text.

personnel security Counterintelligence operations concerned with security clearances and security education.

personnel security authorization and clearance Essentially the same as personnel security clearance.

personnel security clearance A determination by the Department of Defense or an authorized and/or qualified individual that from a security standpoint an individual is eligible for access to classified material of a certain category and all lower categories (also known as personnel security access authorization).

persons of interest   Old spy term for individuals targeted for con games, compromise, "burning," etc.

photo intelligence (PHOTINT)   Intelligence and information gathered from photographic evidence or reconnaissance.

physical security   1) The component of communications security concerned with all physical measures necessary to safeguard communications security material and information from access thereto or observation thereof by unauthorized persons. 2) A protective device against security hazards; physical measures designed to safeguard personnel and to prevent unauthorized access to facilities, material and documents.

PICKLE   President's intelligence checklist; a ten-page newsletter that skims overnight developments of five or six items of concern to the president.

plain component   The sequence of a cipher alphabet containing the plain symbols.

plain coordinates   In cryptography, a sequence of plain digits or letters appearing as one of the two sets of coordinates of a conversation square in an enciphering form.

plain language   *See* plaintext.

plaindress A type of message in which the originator and addressee designations are indicated outside the text. *See* CODRESS.

plaintext Intelligible text or signals that have meaning and that can be read or acted upon without the application of any decryption. Plaintext is usually in the native tongue of the communicators and is the message to be encoded.

plant Sometimes an agent in place or defector in place; but always a reference to an intelligence officer, friendly or hostile, who is in-place within an opposing intelligence service.

plausible denial (PD) The cover for the cover of an intelligence operation. If the operation is blown, it must be plausibly denied that the agency was involved. For example, PD is involved when the Agency gets involved in the funding of an opposition newspaper.

playback system One of the oldest methods of counterespionage extant, this system entails having a double agent transmit to his former employer disinformation supplied by his "new employer." Use of the playback system began in earnest during World War II due to the plethora of captured radio operators on both sides. While throughout history, spies have been "turned," electronic warfare and radio have given us new terminology.

pocket litter The usual litter found in pockets: coins, tickets, keys, etc. In this case, pocket litter is planted so that if the agent is caught, incidental-looking items will reinforce his cover story.

political net   The network of politically sympathetic agents and personnel that can support political operations.

political warfare   Intensified use of political means to achieve a national objective.

polygraph   A controversial electronic device, often called a lie detector or lie box, that supposedly measures human emotional responses, or psychophysical effects, of a subject that might lie while under interrogation. The polygraph is used when interrogating a defector or captured agent, and the CIA routinely uses it for hiring and periodic checkups on existing employees. Business counterespionage officers use the polygraph frequently. Being interviewed with the polygraph is referred to as "being fluttered" or being on the "flutter box."

positive intelligence   Information that can be used in an intelligence report.

practice dangerous to cryptosecurity   A reportable violation of cryptosecurity that, in conjunction with other violations of the same system, may have a considerable adverse effect upon the security of the entire cryptosystem.

prearranged message code   A code adapted to the use of units that require special or technical vocabulary and composed almost exclusively of groups representing complete or nearly complete messages.

president's daily brief   A daily intelligence report given to the president and usually no more than eight or nine staff members. The PDB, as it is referred to, is usually a blue, three-ring loose-leaf book with *President's Daily Brief* on the front. Enclosed in this ten- to fourteen-page report is a top secret summation of the last twenty-four hours of analyzed CIA data. It refers to missiles, mistresses and money, sick despots and Osama bin Laden types. The CIA agent delivering it each morning gives it to eight or nine staffers and the president. Only the president, however, is allowed to keep his copy.

President's Foreign Intelligence Advisory Board (PFIAB) A deliberative and nonauthoritative board formed by President Eisenhower in 1956. The PFIAB had little impact on the day-to-day affairs of the CIA or other intelligence agencies, and in 1977 President Carter disbanded it.

priority A objectives Top-of-the-list mission objectives or intelligence-gathering priorities, especially the latter.

priority code A code or indicator to show that a message or transmission has priority; similar to *urgency designator*.

PRIVATE Private-industry marking assigned to sensitive information, the premature disclosure of which might jeopardize financial planning, manufacturing methods, employee relations, or investigations or which would be detrimental to the best interests of the company or employees concerned.

private code A code made for the exclusive use in correspondence of a group of individuals or a commercial firm. *See also* commercial code.

pro-tex The procedures and techniques used in the actual implementation of security processes within a particular system. A derivative of procedure and techniques, pro-tex designates the means that can be utilized in the actual establishment of a security program.

processing The phase of the intelligence cycle in which information becomes intelligence through recording, evaluation and interpretation.

project An undertaking to 1) develop or procure an item, piece of equipment, system, device, material or component, together with any and all required test facilities including technical buildings, or 2) explore a field in search of knowledge.

project review committee A committee, generally CIA, designed to review all projects costing over a certain amount. This amount varies from year to year.

propaganda Any form of communication designed to influence the opinions, emotions, attitudes or behavior of a group in order to benefit the sponsor either directly or indirectly. There are three types of propaganda:

black Propaganda that purports to emanate from a source other than the true one. An example would be radio propaganda directed to Cuba from a Miami station claiming to be a guerrilla radio station in the Cuban mountains.

gray Propaganda that does not specifically identify the source.

white Propaganda that is disseminated and acknowledged by a sponsor or sponsoring agency.

proprietary A cover corporation or business used by an intelligence agency.

protected information Consists of *classified information* and *other sensitive information*. The definitions below are from the National Security Agency (NSA) but would apply to other agencies as well.

> **classified information** Consists of information classified or classifiable pursuant to the standards of executive order or any successor order, and implementing regulations. It includes, but is not limited to, intelligence and intelligence-related information, sensitive, compartmented (information concerning or derived from intelligence sources and methods) and cryptographic information (information concerning communications security and signals intelligence) protected by Section 798, or Title 18, US Code.

> **other sensitive information** Consists of classified and unclassified information; relating to the organization, functions, activities and personnel of the NSA. It includes, but is not limited to, the names, titles, salaries and numbers of persons employed by or detailed or assigned to the NSA and to communications security information involving codes, ciphers and cryptographic systems used by the US government or any foreign government.

protection area The inner space or volume of a security area rather than the perimeter.

protection, object   System for protecting a specific object such as a safe or file cabinet by the use of a capacitance detector or similar device.

protective security service   A signature security service (*see* signature security) providing constant protection of a shipment between receipt from the consignor until delivery to consignee by one or more carrier custodians. In air movement, observation of the shipment is not required as long as it is stored in a compartment not accessible to any unauthorized person. If accessibility cannot be controlled, the shipment must remain under constant surveillance of an escort or carrier custodian.

provocateur   *See* agents, CIA.

provokatsiya   Russian for the act of provocation.

psyops   The application of propaganda; shortened form of *psychological operations*. Psyops is the planned use of propaganda and other measures to influence the opinions, emotions, attitudes and behavior of hostile, neutral or friendly groups in such a way as to support the achievement of national objectives.

psywar   Now called psyops. *See* above.

psywar net   A network of individuals, stations or units that are in place or emplaced and will function as a communications network of intelligence, psyops, guerrilla operatives or support.

public disclosure   The passing of information and/or materials pertaining to a classified contract to the public or any member of the public by any means of communication.

pucker factor (PF)   A unique physiological factor common to all who have served on covert operations. The PF comes into play when the starboard engine starts to flutter on the 0200 nap-of-the-earth flight or when the one-eyed ethnic type who was your "friendly guide" disappears while leading you on the E&E.

purveyors of the hot poop   The everpresent possessors of hot information that they are willing to sell or exchange for favors.

Q clearance   The type of clearance given to those who work with, have access to and are generally cleared to handle atomic material.

R

random mixed alphabet Alphabet in which the cipher component is constructed by mixing the letters at random.

reading in The process a case officer goes through when he is assigned a new operation or file. To bring himself up to date, he must *read in* all the files on his new assignment.

receipt A written acknowledgment of the change of custody of classified material or documents.

recording The reduction of information to writing or some other form of graphic representation, and the arranging of this information into groups of related items.

red concept The concept that electrical and electronic circuits, components, equipment, systems, etc., that handle

classified plain-language information in electric signal form
(red) be separated from those that handle encrypted or
unclassified information (black). Under this concept, red
and black terminology is used to clarify specific criteria
relating to, and to differentiate between, such circuits,
components, equipments, systems, etc., and the areas in
which they are contained.

red designation   A designation applied to: 1) all wire lines
within the terminal or switching facility carrying classified
plain language; 2) all wire lines between the unencrypted
side of the online cryptoequipment used and individual
subscriber sets or terminal equipment; 3) equipment and
sets originating or terminating classified plain-language
processing equipment; and 4) areas containing these wire
lines and equipment and their interconnecting and auxil-
iary facilities.

red, white and blue work   This term is often used by paramilitary or covert action types when advertising their services; for example, "will only accept red, white and blue
work." By this it is meant that any employment should not
be inimical to Americans or American interests.

reference material   Documentary material over which a
user agency does not have classification jurisdiction and
did not have jurisdiction at the time the material was originated. For example, if the CIA lent documents to the
Department of Defense, DoD could not downgrade this
reference material from TOP SECRET to SECRET because the
department does not have that authority.

registered cryptomaterial Cryptomaterial that is account-able to the office of record and issue on receipt, transfer and destruction, as well as on a quarterly basis.

registered document A classified document bearing a short title and register number for which periodic inventory is established. *See also* registered publication, below.

registered publication A classified publication bearing a register number, as well as a long and short title, and for which periodic accounting is required. *See* registered document.

regrade To classify material up or down (to a higher or lower classification) as protection against unauthorized disclosure.

related missions directive (RMD) A directive that outlines the type of intelligence operations or covert action operations a CIA division can undertake. RMDs are issued to every CIA division on a yearly basis.

release The passage of information to another individual or agency by any means.

repeating key method A method of encipherment using a plurality of alphabets and a key that repeats to indicate the number, identity and sequence of the cipher alphabets employed.

representative of a foreign interest A security term used to describe a foreign or US citizen that is acting as representative, official, agent, etc., of a foreign government. A representative of a foreign interest is not to be confused with a foreign subsidiary in which a US firm has at least 51 percent voting interest.

research and development electronic security The protection resulting from all measures designed to deny to unauthorized persons information of value that might be derived from their interest and study of noncommunications electromagnetic radiations emanating from equipment being developed under the Army Research and Development Program, and all measures taken to ensure that maximum inherent electronic security design features are incorporated into the equipment being developed.

resident director The head of a Soviet spy ring, appointed by Moscow Center after thorough inspection to forestall the possibility of defection. Usually taking up residence illegally in a country bordering the target country, he would seldom be a Soviet but generally an Eastern bloc national. (For example, one could expect to find a Czech running a spy network out of France with West Germany as its target. This would avoid the possibility of embarrassing the Soviets should the network be compromised.) He was assigned a mission of developing a network of spies and funneling all information that his network developed to Moscow Center.

residentura The Soviet KGB or GRU base.

resistance force In unconventional war, that portion of the population of a country engaged in the resistance movement, such as guerrillas.

resistance movement   An organized effort by some portion of the population to resist the established government or occupying power.

restricted area   A controlled area established to safeguard classified material that, because of its size or nature, cannot be adequately protected during working hours by the safeguards prescribed in Department of Defense instructions, but that can be stored during nonworking hours.

restricted data   All data (information) concerning design, manufacture or utilization of atomic weapons; the production of special nuclear material; and the use of special nuclear material in the production of energy.

reverse engineering   Taking apart a product to see how it works; drawing the blueprints in reverse, if you will. Often used in industrial espionage, reverse engineering involves good intelligence work by the company or corporation to get the product before it is patented by the competition. Often a corporation, especially a big cartel, will patent the result of a failed project, a discard, or even a device with a built-in flaw, to throw off the competition. Many a failed product has been patented.

reversed standard alphabet   In cryptography, an alphabet in which the cipher component is in the normal sequence but reversed in direction from the plain component, which is also in normal sequence.

risk category   A compartment or category used to rate or measure the intensity of an operational task.

risk evaluation A study to determine whether the intelligence that can be collected from a high-risk operation is worth the risk.

room circuit In cryptooperations, a circuit that has no connection with outside stations and is used for encipherment and decipherment in an off-line operation.

Royal Canadian Mounted Police (RCMP) One of the best counterespionage units in the world. It was stripped of many duties by an overzealous Canadian Parliament in 1981 because of accusations of civil rights violations. Internal security is now handled by the Security Intelligence Service.

"Run it up a flagpole and see if anybody salutes." Will it (a certain candidacy, idea or thing) work? This expression has become popular among covert-action operatives.

S

S Organization The National Security Agency's Office of Communication Security. One of its functions is to write all the codes used by the United States to protect messages.

sabotage An act with intent to injure, interfere with or obstruct a nation's defense by willfully injuring or destroying or attempting to injure or destroy any national defense material, premises or utilities.

SAD Special Activities Division. A field unit of the CIA. Originally designed to take "Langley's message directly to Osama's cave." Now working to reach out and touch other caveholders as well.

safe house A residence that is used as a meeting place, refuge or network headquarters for intelligence purposes. It is generally deeded to or registered to a "cleared" person who has no trace. It may house communications equipment or other covert operations equipment and may serve as a meeting place for officers and their agents. To preclude observation, access is usually a consideration in developing a safe house.

samizdat The underground movement in the USSR. Usually referred to photocopied, duplicated or printed newspapers passed around to interested parties and groups containing information and news suppressed by the USSR through the state-controlled news sources.

sandbaggers An older British term for covert action operatives. Presumably a term generated by the bag thrown into a leaking dike. In this case, the "leaks" were Soviet operatives during the Cold War.

sanitize To remove all identifying marks and serial numbers so tracing an owner would prove difficult if not impossible. A "sanitized" firearm would be completely anonymous. A sanitary or sanitized operation would be neat and well done as well as untraceable. "By the time the enemy broke into the safe house, it was totally sanitized."

SAP A CIA term for Special Access Program, giving special and niche access to various classified programs to its holder.

Sayeret Motkal Israeli special commandos often used for special or "wet" operations.

schtchit Russian for "shield." A schtchit may be a film showing a mundane beach scene that hides a previously taken photograph of a missile site. If the film were developed by an unaware hostile intelligence, it would find only the beach scene.

SDECE France's Department of Foreign Information and Counterespionage, the French counterpart of the CIA. This organization is not to be confused with the Control of National Surveillance (DST), which is the French counterpart of the FBI. SDECE is considered to be among the top three or four of the world intelligence agencies. The French have not been penetrated as the British have.

SEA Supply Company CIA cover company operating in Southeast Asia in the 1950s. A sister company to Western Enterprises, it was used, mostly in Thailand, for covert activities.

seashell bomb An alleged plot to kill Castro, based on known facts of Castro's penchant for collecting seashells at a certain beach area in Cuba. The plot called for planting a certain very rare shell that would attract Castro's attention. It would explode upon being picked up, or possibly, it would be rigged to explode when lifted from the water and exposed to air.

Second Bureau The English translation of the French Deuxième Bureau.

second secretary The second secretary of a Soviet mission or embassy was usually a KGB officer.

secrecy oath   An oath taken upon employment in most intelligence agencies to preserve and protect classified material the employee would come across in his position of trust.

SECRET   The designation applied only to information or material the unauthorized disclosure of which could reasonably be expected to cause serious damage to national security. For more details, *see* Appendix 2.

secret controlled shipment   SECRET material moving in a commercial carrier, which requires protective security service of a qualified carrier in the interests of national defense. *See* protective security service.

Secret War, CIA's   *See* CIA's Secret War.

secret writing   Codes, ciphers, or cryptography. From Arthur Conan Doyle's *Gloria Scott* to lemon juice and milk, secret writing can be anything or any way to keep people from knowing what you are communicating to a selected individual. There are essentially two kinds of secret writing, wet and dry. *Wet* entails the use of one of various liquids in which an invisible message can be written. Toothpicks or razor edges are used for writing. Then a dummy message is written over the paper in regular, visible ink. Upon receipt, the other party applies a chemical reagent to bring up the hidden message. The *dry* system involves a special "carbon paper" inserted between two ordinary papers. A message is written on the top paper, and upon completion, the top paper and the "carbon" are destroyed. Upon the bottom paper, which appears to be blank, a mundane message is written. Upon receipt, the intended party applies a chemical reagent to bring up the hidden message.

secure phone   Same as a sterile phone, but safer, in that a secure phone cannot be tapped or monitored. *See* sterile phone.

secure room   A room that offers the same or greater security—through the use of guards, alarms or locking devices—than a security container authorized for the storage of classified material. Beyond the book definition, a secure room might also be one that has been debugged or checked for electronic surveillance or taps.

security   Security refers to the safeguarding of information classified TOP SECRET, SECRET or CONFIDENTIAL against unlawful or unauthorized dissemination, duplication or observation.

security briefing and termination   In industrial defense, an employer shall, prior to permitting an employee access to classified information, brief him on his obligation to safeguard classified information, advise him of its importance, inform him of the required security procedure and have him read, or have read to him the portions of the espionage laws, conspiracy laws and federal statutes applicable to the safeguarding of classified information. In addition, the employee shall be advised that he must report to the contractor if he becomes a representative of a foreign interest upon termination of employment. Several forms must be signed upon termination and retained by the contractor.

security cognizance   The responsibility of user agencies for discharging industrial security responsibilities.

Security Intelligence Service   Canadian intelligence service, responsible for counterespionage and internal security. *See* Royal Canadian Mounted Police (RCMP).

security officer   An officer charged with the protection of classified documents, restricted facilities, denied-access areas and, in general, areas or materials put under his charge that if compromised might endanger the security of the United States.

security risk   A broad term covering those that would fail to meet some or all requirements for a security clearance. Some weak points might be homosexuality, foreign-born spouse or relatives and past membership in the Communist party or other groups considered subversive by the Justice Department.

Senior Interagency Group-Intelligence   *See* SIG-I.

sensitive compartmented information   All information and material that requires special controls for restricted handling within compartmented intelligence systems and for which compartmentation is established; also, information concerning or derived from intelligence sources and methods.

sensitive item   Material that requires a high degree of protection because it is fragile, delicate, hazardous to material, or highly technical in nature. Narcotics and special weapons (except ammunition) are examples of sensitive items.

sensitive operations   An operation with an exposure problem for an agency or individual capable of causing embarrassment or even bringing down a government. Usually precise and surgical skill is necessary in a sensitive operation, which may have entailed stealing a valuable document from a Soviet trade delegation or assisting a Bulgarian diplomat to escape his post in East Berlin. Usually a sensitive operation is highly compartmented.

sensitive position   Any position within the Department of the Army that could bring about, by virtue of the nature of the position, a material adverse effect on national security. Such positions include any duty or responsibility that requires access to TOP SECRET, SECRET or CONFIDENTIAL information or material, or any other position so designated by the Secretary of the Army or his designee.

series check   A classified term covering the censoring of National Security Agency (or other agencies) data or information via monitoring so that embarrassing information may be deleted. It would surprise many to learn how much personal comment is passed on the black and back channels of the world's diplomatic services. Comments made by an ambassador to his chief about a delegation head or liaison, like "He has the table manners of a pig" or "His wife is indiscreet" would be weeded out before being sent to the government agency involved.

sheepdipping Placing an officer within an organization for the purpose of establishing credentials that can be used later to penetrate or subvert other groups of like nature.

shellfish toxin Highly potent toxin, such as *Gonyaulax tamarensis*, derived from certain shellfish. Powdered and put in a delivery system, shellfish toxin can be overwhelmingly lethal if delivered correctly.

short title A designation applied to any classified document, material, project or device for purposes of brevity and security. It usually consists of letters or numbers or a combination thereof that will not compromise the subject, substance or classification of the short-titled project. Project White Oak II, for example, may be short-titled *WHOA 2*.

SIG-I These initials stand for Senior Interagency Group-Intelligence. This is the National Security Council's intelligence committee. Its primary function is to deal with intelligence policy, not operations. On 5 August 1982, SIG-I Directive No. 1 was issued, establishing two levels of response to hostile intelligence services. One, the counterintelligence subgroup, is responsible for all countering of "active measures" such as forged US documents and purposefully misleading reports—essentially, counterespionage. The countermeasures subgroup is responsible for electronic countermeasures against technical intrusion such as satellite surveillance and eavesdropping, as well as for the physical security of weapons bases and for the protection of US personnel from enemy attempts at subversion.

signals intelligence (SIGINT) A generic term that includes both communication intelligence and electronic intelligence.

signals security (SIGSEC) A term to describe both communications security and electronic security.

signature security Security designed to provide continuous responsibility for the custody of shipments in transit, so named because a signature and tally are required from each person handling the shipment at each stage of transit from point of origin to destination. Air crews are exempted, as are train crews if the car is sealed.

singleton Spy jargon for an agent or officer working alone, without a chain of support personnel or a network. A singleton has a commercial or deep cover. He is usually capable of high-level contacts, and would report directly to a senior official of the CIA. Sensitive operations would be his forte.

situation report (SITREP) The principal means of reporting to a higher authority information about the tactical situation and such administrative information as may affect the tactical situation.

sleeper An agent placed in a potential target area to await his assignment, which may come years after he is planted. This tactic was often used by Soviets utilizing Eastern bloc refugees that came to the West.

slug (designator) A code name given to a communications unit or transmitting station. To ask "What's your slug?" is to request the designation name of someone's station.

Sluzhba   The political security service of KGB. *Sluzhba* simply means service.

SMERSH   A Soviet intelligence department that specialized in terror outside the borders of the USSR. One of its major goals was to eliminate the national leaders of exiled émigré groups. It was a SMERSH operative that killed Leon Trotsky in Mexico in 1940. SMERSH's laboratory operated twenty-four hours a day to produce some of the world's most deadly toxins, weapons and methods of murder and assassination. The major function of SMERSH was revealed with the defection of two Soviet officers, Khokhlov and Stashinsky.

smoke and mirrors   An old term believed to have originated in circus acts regarding illusions with smoke and mirrors that were used with the main props. Refers to intel work, an older term.

snap report   A preliminary intelligence report of observations by air crews rendered by intelligence personnel immediately following interrogation and dispatched prior to compilation of a detailed mission report.

snuggling   A covert broadcasting technique, used for dissemination of propaganda, that involves radio broadcasting on a frequency just next to the official government one. A station that uses this technique is easily mistaken for the official station on the radio dial. The covert station's frequency is said to snuggle against the real station's frequency.

sociological intelligence Intelligence that deals with the demography, history, development, organization and relationships of groups of people.

soft file Sensitive records that are not filed, yet retained to avoid review by outside sources. They are kept "unofficially," and often stamped *DO NOT FILE*.

soft target A target, whether individual, political, physical or scientific, that offers little defense in the way of security.

source A person, thing or activity from which information is originally obtained.

sourcing Finding the originating point of information; often used in reference to a dummy source. If, for example, a Bulgarian diplomat smuggled to the West a secret Soviet document and the West felt it needed the worldwide publicity, sourcing would come into play. The document could have been leaked to an obscure Belgian paper and, in return for being able to break the story, the editors would not divulge where they got it. Other papers in the area, and eventually the wire services, would pick up the story. The Belgian newspaper became the dummy source. The purpose of sourcing was to protect the original contact, the Bulgarian diplomat, by surfacing the information in a way that would not implicate him.

Southern Air Transport An agency proprietary, based in Miami—or it used to be. Now it is thought to be out of business or to have a new name.

special   Covert, or secret. Any form of warfare with *special* in the title or description can be considered covert or clandestine: special operations, special warfare, special terms, special action group, etc.

special access program   Any program imposing need-to-know or access controls beyond those normally provided for access to TOP SECRET, SECRET, or CONFIDENTIAL information. Such a program includes, but is not limited to, special clearance, adjudication or investigative requirements, special designation of officials authorized to determine need to know, or special lists of persons determined to have a need to know.

SPECIAL ACCESS REQUIRED   Usually a notation placed at least once on material that contains or reveals military space information; designated by the Secretary of the Air Force.

Special Branch   The unit or division of Scotland Yard that makes arrests in all British spy cases. Special Branch relies on MI5 to make the investigation and gather evidence for the arrest. The primary goal of this split function is to protect the identity of the MI5 men by keeping them out of the courts so they won't have to expose themselves by testifying. *See* Military Intelligence 5.

special category messages   Messages identified with specific projects or subjects that require security protection or handling not guaranteed by the normal security classification and require that the message be handled and viewed only by specially cleared or authorized personnel.

Special Committee 303-40   A National Security Council group that approved or disapproved of CIA covert-action operations.

special compartmented intelligence   Intelligence that is compartmented on a need-to-know basis. Often used on special weapons projects such as the Bay of Pigs operation.

Special Forces, US Army   A unique and highly trained unconventional warfare group. Trained primarily to advise and assist the developing forces of other nations, Special Forces have developed into premier counterguerrilla and unconventional warfare specialists.

Special Forces operational base   In unconventional warfare, a provisional organization established within a friendly area by elements of a special forces group to provide command, administration, training, logistical support and intelligence for operational special forces detachments and such other forces that may be placed under its operational control.

Special Group Augmented   A special committee set up and ran by General Edward Lansdale to oversee Operation Mongoose, the plan to "get rid of" Castro that President John Kennedy and Attorney General Robert Kennedy developed.

Special National Intelligence Estimates (SNIES)   Reports issued by the National Security Council that focused attention on a specific area of the world.

special operations (SO)   Since Vietnam, new emphasis—though some say not enough—has been put on special operations as a workable third option. Guerrilla warfare, psyops and E&E are all components of special operations. SO includes, but is not limited to, corrupting and controlling enemy units, indirect or direct action, dissemination of false information, supplying and training friendly forces with lethal weapons and instruments, and general harassment and destruction of the enemy.

Special Operations Group (CIA)   Formed by CIA Director Richard Helms in August 1967, this group was placed in the deputy director of plans' counterintelligence division. Its mission was to provide the Office of Current Intelligence with data on the "peace movement." It was disbanded in late 1968.

Special Operations Group (Joint Chiefs of Staff)   A highly secret team of military personnel composed of US Army Special Forces, Marine Corps Force Recon, Navy SEALs and USAF Special Operations Wing. These units ran high-risk deep-penetration operations in Laos, North Vietnam, Cambodia and other areas. *Special Operations Group* was the original name but the cover name *Studies and Observations Group* was created for media inquiries.

special warfare   Special warfare embraces all the military and paramilitary measures and activities related to unconventional warfare, internal defense and development (counterinsurgency), and psychological operations.

special weapons security   Counterintelligence operations concerned with the security of special weapons systems, ancillary equipment and supporting documents.

spelling group   A code group of which the plain equivalent is a letter or combination of letters used for spelling words not included in the code vocabulary.

spook   Slang for spy or intelligence officer, counterespionage officer or, in general, any espionage agent.

spot   To locate and recruit people with demonstrated access to intelligence targets. This task is given to a PA or agent by a case officer.

spot report   One-time reports used by all echelons to transmit intelligence or information of immediate value.

spy   According to the Hague Convention of 1899, "One who, acting clandestinely or on false pretenses, obtains, or seeks to obtain, information in the zone of operations of a belligerent with the intention of communicating it to a hostile party." This definition would eliminate intelligence analysts, code and cipher clerks, and others in intelligence who are not operatives.

spy dust   A chemical dust composed of nitrophenylpentadienal and referred to as NPPD. Sprayed from an aerosol can, it was used by KGB officers to keep track of American personnel assigned to the US embassy in Moscow. The yellow-white powder was dusted on door knobs, steering wheels and even directly on the clothing of the tracked subject.

spy in the sky A space satellite equipped with electronic surveillance devices. A typical satellite can take a photograph of a license plate from fifty miles up, and every digit will be legible.

spy runner A case officer or agent handler who handles spies.

spy's criteria There are three basic criteria for a good spy: cover, access and language.

squirt transmission Generally a twenty-second burst of apparent noise, which when decoded will contain twenty minutes of information. Sometimes called a *spurt transmission*.

stable Agents controlled by a particular case officer. His list of agents is his "stable."

staff slave A low-ranking minion of an operation. Usually not privy to classified operations.

standard operating procedure (SOP) A set of instructions covering those features of operations that lend themselves to a definite or standardized procedure without loss of effectiveness.

STASI East Germany's old secret police. Disbanded with the fall of the Berlin Wall.

station, CIA   Office of CIA operations generally found in US embassies.

station chief   *See* chief of station.

steganography   The method of concealing the existence of a message by such means as invisible ink, microdots or chemicals. When used for electronic communications, steganography is called transmission security.

sterile phone   A phone that cannot be located even by checking through the telephone company. It can, however, be tapped or monitored.

strategic intelligence   Intelligence that is required for the formation of policy and military plans at national and international levels.

street man   An officer who specializes in meetings, recruitment or clandestine public meetings. Someone good at street tradecraft: surveillance, brush passes, dead drops, etc. "He's a good street man."

stringer   A freelance agent or spy; someone who offers his services as the opportunity arises. As he collects information, he approaches the appropriate party. The stringer is not too dissimilar from a freelance journalist.

strongroom   Usually a room or space within a larger building, separated from the rest of the building by four independent walls and a ceiling. Solidly built, the strongroom is used for the storage of classified material, and is often protected by electronic surveillance devices and alert humans.

Studies and Observations Group   *See* Special Operations Group (Joint Chiefs of Staff).

substitution   In cryptography, the method of converting plaintext into numbers or symbols. "RESTRICTED" may become R O B 56 r8 or 75941.

subversion   1) The lending of support, aid or comfort to groups, individuals or organizations that advocate the over-throw of the US government by force and violence or that are otherwise detrimental to the national security of the United States. 2) Action designed to undermine the military, economic, psychological, moral or political strength of an existing regime.

superencipherment   Result of subjecting cipher text to a further process of encipherment.

superencryption   A further encryption of already encrypted text for increased security.

Supplementary Intelligence Report (SUPINTREP)   A NATO standardized report form used for comprehensive reviews of one or more specific intelligence targets.

surface   To come out of or bring out of deep cover or to reveal a deception. "The Soviets surfaced a long-time in-place agent"; "A dummy agent, used to throw off the counterespionage officers, was surfaced."

surveillance　The systematic observation or monitoring of places, persons or things by visual, aural, electronic, photographic or other means for the purpose of gathering intelligence information.

survival intelligence　The information required by Central Intelligence to operate in the Soviet Union, China or Eastern bloc countries.

syllabary　In a code book, a list of individual letters or of letter or syllable combinations accompanied by their equivalent code groups to be used for spelling out words or proper names not present in the vocabulary of a code. It is sometimes called a "spelling table."

T

tactical signals intelligence (TACSIGINT) A generic term that includes both communications intelligence (COMINT) and electronic intelligence (ELINT).

target study An intelligence study covering all facets of a given target's situation.

Tea and Biscuit Company The CIA: used as slang rather than any attempt at cover.

technical information All information that relates to research, development, engineering, test evaluation, production, operation, use and maintenance of munitions and other military supplies and equipment.

technical intelligence Intelligence concerning technological developments, performance and operational capabilities of foreign material.

technical penetration Electronic surveillance of a target. It can be used to monitor an individual or an opposition operation or organization.

Technical Services Division (TSD) The division within the CIA that produces invisible ink, fountain pen guns and other tradecraft gear. Every nation in the world has a TSD in its intelligence lineup, a very valuable unit of an intelligence agency's skill package.

telephone decoder A device that, when attached to a telephone under surveillance, will make a paper-tape record of the called numbers. Sometimes it is called a pen or pin register. It will record the date, time and length of a call, and whether it is local or long distance.

tempest An unclassified short name referring to investigations and studies compromising emanations. It is sometimes used synonymously with the term "compromising emanations"; for example, tempest tests, tempest inspections, etc.

tempest test A laboratory or on-site (field) test to determine the nature and amplitude of conducted or radiated signals containing compromising information. A test normally includes detection and measurement of these signals and analysis to determine correlation between received signals and potentially compromising transmitted signals.

terminated James Bond fans and the media like to think of this word as the equivalent of assassinated; its true meaning is *dismissed* or *fired from employment*.

textiles, textile business Secret service work. The top-secret research facility at Dimona, Israel, is often referred to as a "textile factory."

Third Agency Rule No US intelligence agency can pass intelligence it receives from one agency to another.

threat study An authoritative intelligence assessment of enemy capabilities in terms of combat materiel, employment doctrine, environment and force structures that would affect general US planning or developments. A threat study has two aspects: an assessment of the level of development that the economy, the technology and/or the forces of a country have achieved or a forecast of what they can be expected to achieve in the future; and a recasting of existing assessments and forecasts that provide a statement of the threat as it relates to a specific research or combat development project.

throughput distribution 1) Shipments that bypass intermediate installations. 2) The bypassing of one or more intermediate supply echelons in the supply system, thereby avoiding multiple handling. Throughput distribution is often used to circumvent normal accounting and shipping records for material to be used for covert operations.

timed drop A pick-up package that will be retrieved by the sender if not picked up in a preset time at the dead drop. A safety precaution.

TOP SECRET A designation applied only to information or material the unauthorized disclosure of which could reasonably be expected to cause exceptionally grave damage to national security. Examples of "exceptionally grave damage" include armed hostilities against the United States and its allies; disruption of foreign relations vitally affecting national security; compromise of vital national defense plans or complex cryptologic and communications intelligence; revelation of sensitive intelligence operations; and the disclosure of scientific or technological developments vital to national security.

top secret control officer An officer, warrant officer or responsible civilian official appointed in each command or agency to be responsible for receipt, custody, accounting of and distribution of TOP SECRET material within the local command and the transmission thereof outside the immediate organization.

tradecraft All skills applicable to the intelligence community, espionage and counterespionage, and spies in general. This would include flaps and seals, surveillance, weapons and other lethal devices, psychological operations, communications, dead drops, etc. Most tradecraft is taught to covert-action operatives that go through the Farm (Camp Peary, Virginia, the CIA's training camp).

traffic Cable traffic or communications volume received during a given period. "Traffic was extremely heavy the day of the Bay of Pigs."

traffic analysis The shifting and sorting of volumes of received communications in cipher or code, or both, in search of clues or messages. A shifting pattern in the military affairs of another country, indicating a change in that country's military deployment, may be discovered through traffic analysis.

transmission Any kind of communication or message, generally electronic.

transposition mixed alphabet Cryptographic alphabet constructed by applying a form of transposition to either a standard or a mixed sequence.

transposition system A code system in which plaintext symbols are retained but are rearranged to form a cryptogram. Essentially, the plaintext is jumbled, so that "RESTRICTED," for example, might be converted to "ICERTSRTDE."

Turkey's Secret Service MIT—Milli Istihbaret Teskilati, National Intelligence Organization.

turn around To double back, change allegiance. "The agent was turned around; he was now a double agent."

turned agent An agent turned by the previously targeted country against his host country. For example, a Russian spy turned around to spy against the Soviets.

two-element differential In certain codes, a difference between the groups of at least two elements, either in the identity or the position occupied. When the elements are letters, the characteristic is called a two-letter differential; when the elements are digits, it is called a two-figure differential.

two-art code   A code consisting of two sections or parts: an encoding section in which the vocabulary items are arranged in alphabetical or other systematic order accompanied by their code equivalents arranged in nonalphabetical or random order, and a decoding section in which the code groups are arranged in alphabetical or numerical order and are accompanied by their plaintext meanings, which are now in mixed order.

Type 97 Cipher Message   A supposedly unbreakable cipher machine developed by the Japanese. By the latter part of 1940, US Army and Navy cryptoanalysts had reconstructed the machine; they were then able to break the Japanese code.

U / V

ultimate intelligence target The enemy's military defense plans.

unauthorized person Any person not authorized to have access to certain classified data or a certain "off-limits" area, in accordance with government or private industry security.

unbound documents Letters, memoranda, reports, telegrams, etc., all of which have temporary or unbound pages.

unconventional warfare (UW) Includes the three interrelated fields of guerrilla warfare, E&E and subversion. UW operations are conducted within enemy or enemy-controlled territory by predominately indigenous personnel, usually supported and directed in varying degrees by an external force.

unconventional warfare operation base A geographical area within enemy or enemy-controlled territory designated by the unified force commander for the conduct of unconventional warfare and related activities in support of theater objectives.

underclassified When documents or other matter are not appropriately protected by assigned classification; "the documents were underclassified."

underground A covert unconventional-warfare organization established to operate in areas denied to the guerrilla forces or to conduct operations not suitable for guerrilla forces.

unvouchered funds General funds that are free from any kind of review by the usual agencies, the General Accounting Office, IRS, General Services Administration or even Congress. There are several small House or Senate subcommittees that in theory have access to unvouchered expenditures. The executive branch has access to knowledge of these unvouchered funds at any time but seldom exercises the privilege.

unwitting agent People in target areas or countries who unknowingly serve as conduits for intelligence or are used in the operational efforts of covert-action officers. A typical unwitting agent might be an editor of a newspaper, a local politician or anybody else with access to important people. This person will be fed information in such a way that the sponsor remains anonymous and the information appears innocuous. The net effort will be directed at discrediting the local communist organization or general opposition.

upgrade To raise the classification of protected material. The most important part of the process is notifying the possessors of the material of the upgrading in order to avoid compromise of now more protected matter.

upravlyayushchii Literally, director. It was the title used within the various directorates and departments of the KGB.

UPS An abbreviation for "uncontested physical searches," a soft term for black-bag jobs or break-ins.

urgency designator A code or letter prefix used on electronic communications to designate the priority of a given message and the precedence it is to be accorded on the wire.

US counterinsurgent forces Special action forces and other US Army units, elements or personnel trained and designated for a counterinsurgent mission. These forces are capable of operating in vulnerable areas when invited by a host government and providing training and military advice and operational assistance to indigenous military and paramilitary forces engaged in maintaining or restoring internal security and defeating subversive insurgency.

user agency Those government agencies involved with intelligence use, including but not limited to the FBI, CIA, Drug Enforcement Agency, army, air force, navy, NASA, and the Departments of State, Justice, Labor and Defense.

Uvedomlatni Otdel The unit within the Soviet KGB's First Chief Directorate that was charged with communicating to the hierarchy all results of Soviet covert activities. This information was usually presented raw and without analysis although the unit had an analysis section.

vault   Any room, compartment or area that has a secure access area. Usually the walls must be of masonry extending from the floor to the floor above. Ceiling and floor must offer the same resistance as the walls. The doors must be drill-resistant steel, and, if classified documents are kept, the room should have a sprinkler system. Security may be enhanced by the use of at least two independent electronic security systems.

vet   To appraise, treat or eliminate. The British use this term in reference to purging an agency or bureau. In the United States, to vet a potential agent is to test him.

Vietnamese Air Transport Corporation (VIAT)   A cover or notional business set up by CIA director William Colby to supply and service clandestine operations against the North Vietnamese. Colby thought Air America was too compromised for the job.

Vigenere table   A cipher square, commonly attributed in cryptographic literature to the French crypto expert, Vigenere. It consists of a square having the normal sequence at the top (or at the bottom) and at the left or right, and cyclic permutations of the normal sequence forming the successive rows or columns within the square. The term is sometimes applied to a square exhibiting such symmetry but with a mixed sequence.

vocoder A type of voice coder consisting of a speech analyzer and a speech synthesizer used to reduce the bandwidth requirement of speech signals. The analyzer circuitry converts the incoming analog speech-wave form into narrow and digital signals. The synthesizer converts the encoded digital output of the received component into artificial speech sounds. For communications security (COMMSEC) purposes, a vocoder may be used in conjunction with a key generator and a modulator-demodulator device to transmit digitally encrypted speech signals over normal narrow-band voice communication channels.

vulnerability paragraph In a target study or target analysis, a paragraph that is earmarked for explaining vulnerabilities in an operation, which could possibly be exploited by the enemy. This information is always highly classified.

W / X / Y / Z

W.H. Division   CIA designation for Western Hemisphere Division.

walk-in   A reference to a member of a local communist party or front group that comes into an American embassy to offer his services to the United States. His reason may be genuine political disillusionment, a need for cash or simply a desire for excitement. US Marine security guards as well as secretaries in the mission are very alert to this sort of person. Often appearing nervous and very suspicious, he will be handled carefully by a legitimate officer of the Department of State. Should the walk-in's bona fides check out, another meeting will be set up with a local CIA officer. Many walk-ins will insist on talking only to the station chief or an officer.

Walnut   Project name for an IBM computer data-retrieval system. Out of billions of pieces of information, Walnut could retrieve such details as the kind of wood Soviet carpenters were using to create weapons, the kind of car a CIA officer applicant had when he was sixteen, or the name of Khrushchev's first girlfriend. Walnut was the heart of the CIA's massive information bank.

wars of national liberation The propaganda term used by communists to dignify and lend legitimacy to covert aggression.

watchlist A list of sensitive subjects: people, places and things. Watchlist information is programmed into computers, which will reveal the sensitive subject should it turn up while data is being input or reviewed.

weapon system A weapon and all of its support components.

Western Enterprises Commercial cover name for a CIA and Chinat (Chinese Nationalist) operation to invade Yunnan Province of mainland China via Burma; operational in the early 1950s.

wet work, wet affairs, wet operations A Soviet term (in Russian, *mokrie dela*) for assassination and violence; generally came under the direction of Department V of the KGB Directorate.

WHITE STAR The code name for a covert operation in Laos from late 1959 to 1962 to help the Lao royalists and the Lao neutralists to fight off the Pathet Lao guerrillas. The first commander of the WHITE STAR team of Special Forces personnel was Colonel Arthur "Bull" Simmons. *See* CIA's Secret War.

Wise Old Men   A name sometimes applied to the senior informal advisory group that advised President Johnson.

witting agent   One who knowingly works for an intelligence agency, officer or local station. *See* unwitting agent.

work in progress   Classified material being made ready for typing and/or final reproduction. Documents consist of rough drafts, photos, notes and so on that precede release of classified finished matter.

worst casing   Advance planning for a "worst case," for the worst possible hitch in an operation. Should a flap develop or the project or operation get blown for some reason, any team that has done its worst casting will have an alternative extraction plan or contingency plans.

zone   A certain division within a security area or nonaccess area. A zone usually contains several intrusion detector devices monitored by a station that is manned by an individual or, if it is a nuclear center, by a team.

Appendix 1

EVALUATION OF INTELLIGENCE

Evaluation of intelligence includes the determination of the pertinence and accuracy of the information, reliability of the source and the agency through which the information was collected or derived.

1. How does the information relate to the enemy or to the characteristics of the area of operations?
2. Is the information needed immediately, and if so, by whom?
3. Does the information have present or future value, and if so, to whom?

The principal basis for judging the reliability of a source or an agency is previous experience. The training, experience and past performance of the collecting agency and the source are also taken into consideration. A collecting agency closest to the source is ordinarily the best judge of the reliability of the information and the source. Consequently, a higher echelon of the collecting agency should normally accept the reliability evaluation of the lower and closer agency unit. In reality, however, more often than it should happen, the higher agency echelon disregards the lower agency's recommendation and pursues a contrary course of action.

Accuracy refers to the probable truth of the information. A judgment of accuracy is based on the following:

1. Is it possible for the reported fact or event to have taken place?
2. Is the report consistent within itself?
3. Is the report confirmed or corroborated by information from different sources or agencies?
4. Does the report agree or disagree in any way with other available information?
5. If the report does not agree with information from other sources or agencies, which one is more likely to be true?

The most reliable method of judging the accuracy of a report is by comparing it with similar information that may already be available under the proper category in an intelligence file or workbook. Ideally, the intelligence officer or analyst obtains information through different agencies and/or many sources.

Often, this is where the difference occurs between a higher echelon of the collection agency and the lower unit. Usually the echelon at the higher level has more opportunity for a greater range of collection sources and will often arrive at a different conclusion simply by having more input on a given subject. The higher echelon's greater ability to confirm, corroborate or refute the accuracy of various reports gives it more judgmental leeway.

The evaluation of each item of information has been standardized by a letter and numeral system. For reliability, a letter is used and for accuracy, a numeral.

For evaluation of the reliability of a source and collection agency, a rating is used as follows:

A—Completely reliable
B—Usually reliable
C—Fairly reliable
D—Not usually reliable
E—Unreliable
F—Reliability cannot be judged.

The "A" rating is used only under the most unusual circumstances. A "B" would indicate a source of known integrity, and an "F" would be used when there is no adequate basis for estimating the reliability of the source.

Higher echelons will rate the lower collecting agency just as that lower agency rates the source of the original information. Should the lower agency rate the source as a "C," but the higher echelon rate the agency a "D," then only the lower degree of reliability is indicated.

Accuracy evaluation is based on numerals as indicated:

1—Confirmed by other sources
2—Probably true
3—Possibly true
4—Doubtfully true
5—Improbable
6—Truth cannot be judged.

Although both letters and numerals are used to indicate the evaluation of an item of information, they are independent of each other. A completely reliable agency may report information obtained from a completely reliable source that, on the basis of other information, is judged to be improbable. In this case the information would be rated A-5. On the other hand, a source known in the past to be completely unreliable may provide raw information that, after confirmation by reliable sources, is accepted as accurate and should not be discarded out of hand.

This is a basic method and should not be considered the end-all of verification and evaluation. Far more sophisticated methods are available to those in analysis and intelligence gathering for information verification. These range from extensive questioning and interrogation of a defector, both for his information and to discover his bona fides, to triangulation, a classic method of intelligence detective work.

Appendix 2

EQUIVALENT SECURITY CLASSIFICATIONS OF FOREIGN COUNTRIES AND INTERNATIONAL PACT ORGANIZATIONS

Every country in the world has a system to classify and protect its valued documents. While the protective systems and methods used to safeguard this material vary greatly, the intent is the same.

The classification systems vary in that what is considered TOP SECRET in this country may be shared with another country where it is handled in a less than safeguarded fashion. Dissemination codes such as NOFORN (no foreign) on certain data will, therefore, often govern who gets to see what, even among "trusted" allies.

Equivalent Security Classifications

COUNTRY	TOP SECRET	SECRET	CONFIDENTIAL	OTHER
Argentina	ESTRICTAMENTE SECRETO	SECRETO	CONFIDENCIAL	RESERVADO
Australia	TOP SECRET	SECRET	CONFIDENTIAL	RESTRICTED
Austria	STRENG GEHEIM	GEHEIM	VERSCHLUSS	
Belgium French	TRÈS SECRET	SECRET	CONFIDENTIEL	DIFFUSION RESTREINTE
Flemish	ZEER GEHEIM	GEHEIM	VERTROUWELIJK	BEPERTKE VERSPREIDING
Bolivia	SUPERSECRETO or MUY SECRETO	SECRETO	CONFIDENCIAL	RESERVADO
Brazil	ULTRA SECRETO	SECRETO	CONFIDENCIAL	RESERVADO
Cambodia	TRÈS SECRET	SECRET	SECRET/CONFIDENTIEL	N/A
Canada	TOP SECRET	SECRET	CONFIDENTIAL	RESTRICTED
Chile	SECRETO	SECRETO	RESERVADO	RESERVADO
Colombia	ULTRASECRETO	SECRETO	RESERVADO	CONFIDENCIAL RESTRINGIDO
Costa Rica	ALTO SECRETO	SECRETO	CONFIDENCIAL	N/A

Denmark	HOJST HIMMILIGT	HIMMILIGT	FORTROLIGT	TIL TJENESTEBRUG
Ecuador	SECRETESIMO	SECRETO	CONFIDENCIAL	RESERVADO
El Salvador	ULTRA SECRETO	SECRETO	CONFIDENCIAL	RESERVADO
Ethiopia	YEMIAZ BIRTOU MISTIR	MISTIR	KILKIL	N/A
Finland	ERITTAIN SALAINEN	SALAINEN	N/A	N/A
France	TRÈS SECRET	SECRET DEFENSE	CONFIDENTIEL DEFENSE	DIFFUSION RESTREINTE
Germany	STRENG GEHEIM	GEHEIM	VS-VERTRAULICH	N/A
Guatemala	ALTO SECRETO	SECRETO	CONFIDENCIAL	RESERVADO
Haiti	N/A	SECRET	CONFIDENTIAL	N/A
Honduras	SUPER SECRETO	SECRETO	CONFIDENCIAL	RESERVADO
Hong Kong	TOP SECRET	SECRET	CONFIDENTIAL	RESTRICTED
Hungary	SZIGORUAN TITKOS	TITKOS	BIZLAMAS	N/A
Iceland	ALGJORTI	TRUNADARMAL		
India	TOP SECRET	SECRET	CONFIDENTIAL	RESTRICTED
Indonesia	SANGAT RAHASIA	RAHASIA	TERBATAS	N/A
Iran	BEKOLI SERRI	SERRI	KHEILI MAHRAMANEH	MAHRAMANEH

Equivalent Security Classifications

COUNTRY	TOP SECRET	SECRET	CONFIDENTIAL	OTHER
	(absolutely secret)	(secret)	(confidential)	(limited)
Iraq				
Ireland	TOP SECRET	SECRET	CONFIDENTIAL	RESTRICTED
Gaelic	AN-SICREIDEACH	SICREIDEACH	RUNDA	SRIANTA
Israel	SODI BEYOTER	SODI	SHAMUR	MUGBAL
Italy	SEGRETISSIMO	SEGRETO	RISERVATISSIMO	RISERVATO
Japan	KIMITSU	GOKUHI	HI	TORIATSUKAICHUI
Jordan	MAKTUM JIDDAN	MAKTUM	SIRRI	MAHDUD
Korea	111 KUP PI MIL	11 KUP PI MIL	1 KUP PI MIL	N/A
Laos	TRÉS SECRET	SECRET	CONFIDENTIEL	N/A
Lebanon	TRÉS SECRET	SECRET	CONFIDENTIEL	N/A
Mexico	ALTO SECRETO	SECRETO	CONFIDENCIAL	RESTRINGIDO
Netherlands	ZEER GEHEIM	GEHEIM	CONFIDENTIEEL or VERTROUWELIJK	DIENSTGEHEIM
New Zealand	TOP SECRET	SECRET	CONFIDENTIAL	RESTRICTED
Nicaragua	ALTO SECRETO	SECRETO	CONFIDENCIAL	RESERVADO
Norway	STRENGHT HEMMELIG	HEMMELIG	KONFIDENEIELT	BEGRENSET
Pakistan	TOP SECRET	SECRET	CONFIDENTIAL	RESTRICTED
Paraguay	SECRETO	SECRETO	CONFIDENCIAL	RESERVADO

Peru	ESTRICTAMENTE SECRETO	SECRETO	CONFIDENCIAL	RESERVADO
Philippines	TOP SECRET	SECRET	CONFIDENTIAL	RESTRICTED
Portugal	MUITO SECRETO	SECRETO	CONFIDENCIAL	RESERVADO
Spain	MAXIMO SECRETO	SECRETO	CONFIDENCIAL	DIFFUSSION LIMITADA
Sweden (red borders)	HEMLIG	HEMLIG		

Switzerland (three languages): TOP SECRET has a registration number to distinguish it from SECRET and CONFIDENTIAL)

French	TRÈS SECRET	SECRET DEFENSE	CONFIDENTIEL DEFENSE	DIFFUSION RESTREINTE
German	STRENG GEHEIM	GEHEIM	VERTRAULICH	N/A
Italian	SEGRETISSIMO	SEGRETO	RISERVATISSIMO	RISERVATO
Thailand	LUP TISUD	LUP MAAG	LUP	POK PID
Turkey	COK GIZLI	GIZLI	OZEL	HIZMETE OZEL
Union of South Africa				
English	TOP SECRET	SECRET	CONFIDENTIAL	RESTRICTED
Afrikaans	UTTERS GEHEIM	GEHEIM	VERTROULIK	BEPERK
United Arab Republic	TOP SECRET	VERY SECRET	SECRET	OFFICIAL

Equivalent Security Classifications

COUNTRY	TOP SECRET	SECRET	CONFIDENTIAL	OTHER
United Kingdom	TOP SECRET	SECRET	CONFIDENTIAL	RESTRICTED
Uruguay	ULTRA SECRETO	SECRETO	CONFIDENCIAL	RESERVADO
USSR	СОВЕРСШННО СЕКРЕТНО	СЕКРЕТНО	НЕ ПОДЛЕЖИЙ ОГЛАШЕННЮ	ДЛЯ СЛჄЖЕБНОГО ПОЛЬЗОВАННЯ
Vietnam French	TRÉS SECRET	SECRET DEFENSE	CONFIDENTIAL DEFENSE	DIFFUSION RESTREINTE
Vietnamese	TÔI-MÂT	MÂT	KIN	TU MÂT
NATO	COSMIC TOP SECRET	NATO SECRET	NATO CONFIDENTIAL	NATO RESTRICTED

Foreign security classification systems are not always parallel to the U.S. system, and so exact equivalent classifications cannot be given. The classifications above represent the nearest comparable designations to those prescribed for U.S. classification.

"ATOMAL" information is an exclusive designation used by NATO to identify Restricted Data or Formerly Restricted Data information released by the United States to NATO.

There is no Swedish security classification equal to U.S. CONFIDENTIAL, hence all Swedish information or material received by the United States and classified HEMLIG will be safeguarded as U.S. SECRET. U.S. information or material received by the Swedish government and classified CONFIDENTIAL will be safeguarded as HEMLIG.

Appendix 3

THE INTELLIGENCE CYCLE

The Intelligence Cycle

is the process by which information is acquired, converted into intelligence, and made available to policy makers. There are usually five steps that constitute *The Intelligence Cycle*.

1. Planning and Direction

This involves the management of the entire effort, from the identification of the need for data to the final delivery of an intelligence product to a customer.

The whole process is initiated by requests or requirements for intelligence on certain subjects. These are based on the ultimate needs of the policy makers—the president, the National Security Council, and other major departments and agencies of government.

2. Collection

This involves the gathering of the raw data from which finished intelligence will be produced. There are many sources for the collection of information, including foreign radio-broadcasts, newspapers, periodicals and official government personnel stationed in American embassies abroad.

There are also secret sources, such as agents and defectors who provide information obtainable in no other way.

Finally, technical collection—photography and electronics—has come to play an indispensable part in modern intelligence by extending the United States' sensory system—its eyes and ears.

3. Processing

This step is concerned with the conversion of the vast amount of information coming into the system to a form more suitable for the production of finished intelligence, such as language translations, decryption and sorting by subject matter. The information that does not go directly to analysts is sorted and made available for rapid computer retrieval.

Processing also refers to data reduction—interpretation of the information stored on film and tape through the use of highly refined photographic and electronic processes.

4. Production and Analysis

This refers to the conversion of basic information into finished intelligence. It includes the integration, evaluation and analysis of all available data and the preparation of a variety of intelligence products. Such products or estimates may be presented as briefings, brief reports or lengthy studies.

The "raw intelligence" collected is frequently fragmentary and at times contradictory. Analysts, who are subject-matter specialists for a particular country, produce finished intelligence by evaluating and integrating the various pieces of data and interpreting their meaning and significance.

The subjects involved may concern different regions, problems or personalities in various contexts—political, geographic, economic, military, scientific or biographic. Current events, capabilities or probable developments in the future may also be examined.

5. Dissemination

The last step is the distribution and handling of the finished intelligence to the consumers of intelligence, the same policy makers whose needs triggered the Intelligence Cycle.

Sound policy decisions must be based on sound knowledge. Intelligence aims to provide that knowledge.

Appendix 4

THE INTELLIGENCE COMMUNITY

Throughout this book, the phrase "intelligence community" has been used with frequency. I hope this section will explain the meaning of this exact wording.

The leader of the intelligence community is at the same time the head of the CIA. Yet the CIA is but one component of the intelligence community (IC). The IC refers to the aggregate of those executive branch agencies and organizations that conduct the intelligence activities that comprise the total US national intelligence effort. The community includes the:

- Central Intelligence Agency
- National Security Agency
- Defense Intelligence Agency
- Bureau of Intelligence and Research of the Department of State
- Intelligence elements of the military services
- Federal Bureau of Investigation
- Department of the Treasury
- Department of Energy

- Those offices within the Department of Defense that collect specialized national foreign intelligence through reconnaissance programs
- Members of the intelligence community staff

The various cited members of the IC advise the director of the CIA through their members on the various specialized committees that deal with intelligence matters of common concern. Chief among these groups is the National Foreign Intelligence Board, which the director chairs.

The Intelligence Community

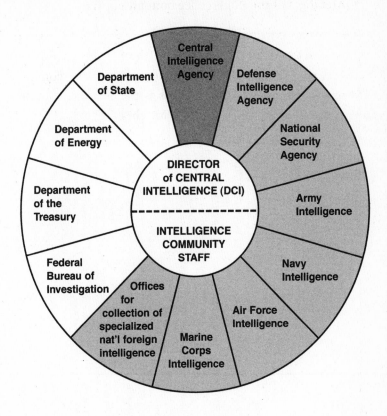

- Department of Defense Elements
- Departmental Intelligence Elements (Other than DoD)
- Independent Agency

Director of Central Intelligence Command Responsibilities

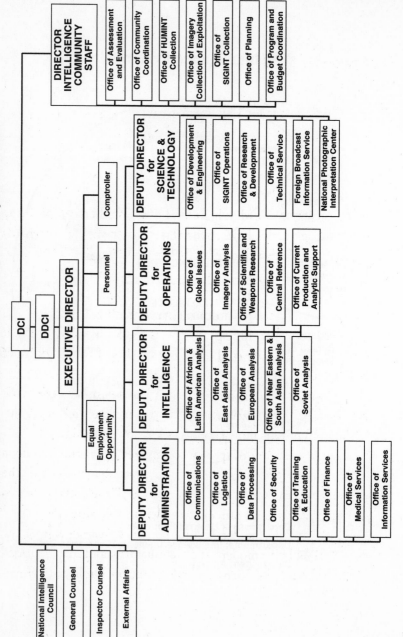

DCI

DDCI

National Intelligence Council

General Counsel

Inspector Counsel

External Affairs

EXECUTIVE DIRECTOR

Equal Employment Opportunity

Personnel

Comptroller

DIRECTOR INTELLIGENCE COMMUNITY STAFF
- Office of Assessment and Evaluation
- Office of Community Coordination
- Office of HUMINT Collection
- Office of Imagery Collection of Exploitation
- Office of SIGINT Collection
- Office of Planning
- Office of Program and Budget Coordination

DEPUTY DIRECTOR for ADMINISTRATION
- Office of Communications
- Office of Logistics
- Office of Data Processing
- Office of Security
- Office of Training & Education
- Office of Finance
- Office of Medical Services
- Office of Information Services

DEPUTY DIRECTOR for INTELLIGENCE
- Office of African & Latin American Analysis
- Office of East Asian Analysis
- Office of European Analysis
- Office of Near Eastern & South Asian Analysis
- Office of Soviet Analysis

DEPUTY DIRECTOR for OPERATIONS
- Office of Global Issues
- Office of Imagery Analysis
- Office of Scientific and Weapons Research
- Office of Central Reference
- Office of Current Production and Analytic Support

DEPUTY DIRECTOR for SCIENCE & TECHNOLOGY
- Office of Development & Engineering
- Office of SIGINT Operations
- Office of Research & Development
- Office of Technical Service
- Foreign Broadcast Information Service
- National Photographic Interpretation Center

Appendix 5

PERSONA NON GRATA

A spy is caught. So what happens next? Should a captured spy or espionage agent have a diplomat's cover such as the KGB had, he will be expelled from the United States.

Since it seems that every KGB officer had a cover as a second secretary at the Soviety Embassy, the usual procedure was service of an expulsion order, a declaration of *persona non grata*. If, however, the spy was a singleton working without diplomatic cover, he could literally be shot if found guilty of espionage.

Diplomatic cover is more abused than any other diplomatic courtesy. With the exception of unpaid parking tickets, diplomatic immunity is most often invoked for espionage.

Should a network of spies be uncovered operating in Silicon Valley, the only recourse the United States has is to expel the spies from the country. Of course, this is all the Russians could do to our agents and officers in a comparable situation.

The provision for declaring a person *persona non grata* has been codified into modern international law and may be found in Article 9 of the Vienna Convention on Diplomatic Relations of 1961.